P9-DGK-378

LISA SAMSON AND TY SAMSON

Love MERCY

A Mother & Daughter's Journey from The American Dream to the Kingdom of God

ZONDERVAN®

ZONDERVAN.com/
AUTHORTRACKER
follow your favorite authors

JESSAMINE COUNTY PUBLIC LIBRARY
600 South Main Street
Nicholasville, KY 40356
(859) 885-3523

ZONDERVAN

Love Mercy
Copyright © 2010 by Lisa Samson and Ty Samson

This title is also available as a Zondervan ebook.
Visit www.zondervan.com/ebooks.

This title is also available in a Zondervan audio edition.
Visit www.zondervan.fm.

Requests for information should be addressed to:
Zondervan, *Grand Rapids, Michigan 49530*

Library of Congress Cataloging-in-Publication Data

Samson, Lisa, 1964-
    Love mercy : a mother and daughter's journey from the American dream to the
    kingdom of God / Lisa Samson and Ty Samson.
        p. cm.
    ISBN 978-0-310-28477-2 (softcover)
    1. Samson, Lisa, 1964 – Travel – Africa. 2. Authors, American – Travel – Africa. 3.
Mothers and daughters – United States – Biography. 4. Voyages and travels – Religious
aspects – Christianity. 5. Christian biography. I. Samson, Ty, 1989- II. Title.
PS3569.A46673Z46 2010
818'.54 – dc22
    [B]   2009026492

All Scripture quotations, unless otherwise indicated, are taken from the Holy Bible, *New
International Version®, NIV®.* Copyright © 1973, 1978, 1984 by Biblica, Inc.™ Used by permission of Zondervan. All rights reserved worldwide.

Any Internet addresses (websites, blogs, etc.) and telephone numbers printed in this book
are offered as a resource. They are not intended in any way to be or imply an endorsement
by Zondervan, nor does Zondervan vouch for the content of these sites and numbers for
the life of this book.

All rights reserved. No part of this publication may be reproduced, stored in a retrieval
system, or transmitted in any form or by any means – electronic, mechanical, photocopy,
recording, or any other – except for brief quotations in printed reviews, without the prior
permission of the publisher.

Cover design: *Juicebox Designs*
Interior design: *Christine Orejuela-Winkelman*
Interior photographs: *Copyright E. Tyler Samson*

Printed in the United States of America

09 10 11 12 13 14 15 • 22 21 20 19 18 17 16 15 14 13 12 11 10 9 8 7 6 5 4 3 2 1

3 2530 60665 8498

For Tom,
for leading the way,
and Dennis,
fearless leader of "Sunny D and B.A.H.s"

CONTENTS

PART 2: JOURNEY TO AFRICA

PART 3: BACK IN LEXINGTON

A NOTE TO OUR READERS

When the call that would change my life came from my agent, I had no idea that's what it was.

"Lisa, it's Don. A friend of mine wants to write a novel. He's a great guy, it's a great story, but he needs some help. Can you talk to him on the phone?"

"Sure."

When Tom Davis, the president of Children's HopeChest, phoned a few days later, I was sitting with my friend Leigh on her screened porch. I was in Maryland for a summer visit, and it seemed justice was following me back home, and an opportunity to help a budding novelist would turn into something far more life-giving to me than it would ever be to Tom.

We discussed his story, engaging right away in talk of the need for conflict, the importance of the setting, and the keys to developing memorable characters. Sometimes, you talk to someone, and you just know they're your kind of people. Immediately I felt a rapport with Tom, and soon, due to the fact his novel was about an icon found in Russia, we began talking about his work with orphans. Children's HopeChest had been providing much-needed care and service to orphans in Russia for several years. It was obvious he loved the country and its people.

"We're heading into Swaziland," Tom said, telling me about the need in Africa.

We soon began talking frequently about his book, and when he was offered a book deal for a series of books about orphans, he visited for long editing sessions, food provided by my husband, Will, of course.

One day, Tom told me about a vision trip to Swaziland. "You should come." Tom surrounds himself with people—a well-meaning entourage

—who aren't afraid to see the hard things of the world, people capable of looking beyond their borders and taking their faith to the whole world, no matter how hard that might be.

I thought about it. Thought about how much it would cost. Thought about how much our seventeen-year-old daughter, Ty, would love a trip like this.

"Let me get more information," I told him, and a few days later the emails began to arrive. Swazi culture. Fund-raising tips. The great work Children's HopeChest was doing, and wanted to do, in the tiny kingdom of Swaziland.

Hmm. Maybe I could make jewelry to sell. Maybe I could dip into the kids' college fund. Maybe, maybe, maybe ... anything! But don't ask me to raise support. I'm a proud woman, unfortunately, and sending out letters just isn't in me.

Meanwhile, Tom kept asking. "We have a trip coming up next January. You in?"

"I dunno ..."

"Oh, come on, Lisa! You'll love it."

Of course I would.

A lightbulb eventually went on. I called Tom. "What if I put together a book proposal? I could write a book about the trip, and the advance would pay our way and the rest could go to Children's HopeChest."

"That's a great idea! Not only would it get you here, but your book would raise awareness."

I immediately put together a three-page proposal and sent it off to my agent, and he began shopping it around. A book. Nonfiction. A new way of writing. Could I do it? And Africa? Really? I'd been to England, but that was it. I wasn't a well-traveled person at all.

Tom's excitement grew. "This is going to be great. A lot of the trips concentrate on going to our carepoints where we feed the kids, but I want you to see as much as possible. This will be a vision trip more than a mission trip. You can see what the people are going through and tell others."

It sounded like the perfect plan. If only I could find a publishing house that would take a chance. Lisa Samson writes novels. She does not write about her life, about trips to Africa with her daughter. In this day of bottom-line sales, would someone catch the vision, see the possibilities? We could only hope and pray.

Obviously, you know what happened.

PRELUDE: HEADING TO SWAZILAND

⌒⊙⌒⊙⌒

LISA

After church today, my husband, Will, cooked up a shepherd's pie to remember. He filled it with locally grown beef and sausage and added great dollops of local, organically grown mashed potatoes on top. Last came handfuls of cheddar cheese (from Kroger, but hey, local cheese is expensive!), and then he baked it in our oven, filling every room in our house with a tempting, savory smell. When at last it was ready to eat, everyone devoured two helpings, except for Jake, our thirteen-year-old son — he ate three.

Later that afternoon, we ate some of Ty's homemade pumpkin bread. She's the expert baker around our home, supplying us with from-scratch bread that she kneads by hand. We don't eat fancy around here, but we do eat healthy — which is the best luxury of all.

Despite the abundance of good food, on occasion I skip a meal, and that, too, is a luxury. Skipping a meal means I had a choice. *I* decided there was too much of me around the middle. *I* decided that since plenty of food waited in the refrigerator, I could turn my back on it and have a cup of tea instead. The food would be waiting for me. I've never once thought, "I'd better eat this now. I don't know where my next meal is coming from."

My food is easy to come by. No walking for miles and miles. There are always some tasty leftovers in the fridge, or cereals and soups in the pantry. My husband is the chef and the shopper — all I have to do is enjoy his provision.

My days are simple. When I wake up, I make a cup of tea, surf the Internet for a while, read email, and grab the mail from the box attached to our large old house in downtown Lexington. After throwing on clothes with no holes in them — if something does have a hole, I take hours to sew on a funky patch — I head to church for daily Mass, where I sit among friends in climate-controlled comfort. At least one day a week, I meet a friend for lunch at Al's Bar and Grill. (I usually get the hamburger special with homemade sweet potato fries.) For dinner, Will makes pasta or grills fish or chicken. Our vegetables usually come from the farmer's market, our garden, or our share in a nearby CSA (community-supported agriculture) farm.

We are rich.

We don't go on expensive vacations. We buy most of our clothing used. We don't get our nails done, and we're thankful for my niece, who does our hair when we visit because a full-on trip to the salon is out of our reach. Nice meals out are reserved for birthdays and special occasions. We keep our heat down to 60 degrees in the winter to lower our utility bills.

But we are rich.

According to *globalrichlist.com*, my family and I are richer than over 80 percent of the rest of the world's inhabitants.

Pinned to the wall beside the desk where I write are two pictures taken in Sudan in 1993. The first shows a man reduced to a skeleton, his thighs no more than twelve inches in circumference, his lips pulled back from his teeth, the skin of his face shrink-wrapped around his skull. He is crawling in the dirt outside a feeding tent. The second picture is a little girl, no more than two years old, her legs drawn up beneath her as she crouches on the ground, her hands cradling her head as her forehead rests on the ground. A buzzard waits in the background.

When I look at these pictures, all that is in me cries out, "Why, Lord?" I believe I will wrestle with that question until I can ask God face-to-face. In the meantime, I read the Holy Scriptures and find verse upon verse upon verse that implore me, command me, to pick up that little girl and help that man. I long to say yes.

But my life is busy. I've got organic shepherd's pie to eat, fair trade clothing to buy, and books about justice to write. Who has the time for anything more than wishing?

God, have mercy on me in my busyness. God, have mercy on me, a woman who has time to surf the Internet while my brothers and sisters are pulled into the arms of death.

Is this the only life a rich person can lead?

There came a moment—an ordinary moment in the midst of my comfortable routine—when the cognitive dissonance simply became too great. The reality of my daily choices was simply too far removed from the injunctions of Scripture. In that moment I understood that something had to change.

So I'm going to Swaziland.

What will I find? What will it be like to squat in the dirt beside orphans, beside men, women, and children being killed by AIDS and starvation? *Dear Lord, help me hold it together—I don't want to cry the whole time. Dear Lord, I will go to your children because you ask me to; I will hold your tiny wailing babies.*

How can I do this? What can I offer the people of Swaziland from out of my comfort, luxury, and self-absorption? Why am I going?

I'm going because my Jesus asks me to feed the hungry, clothe the naked, and care for the sick. I'm going because it's right. I'm going to help people who are dying because I know that to stay where I am is a kind of slow death.

I'm going. For the love of God I'm going.

෯෨෨෯

TY

A few autumns ago, I began working at the Catholic Action Center (CAC), an inner-city ministry to the homeless and the poor here in Lexington. I wasn't sure what I would do or who I would meet, but I had to do something to reach outside myself, to figure out what faith means when more than belief comes into play.

Three days of volunteering slowly became five and eventually six.

When I first started, I loved it. I interacted with people in need, some who were thankful and some who weren't. I did their laundry and chatted about their day. Even sorting through items for us to give away gave me a sense of satisfaction in knowing someone would need the coat I was inspecting or the pair of pants I was folding. But soon it began to feel like a boring, regular office job. I'd signed up because I didn't want to be one of the people complaining about injustice but never lifting a finger, and now I found myself doing nothing more than running errands, making copies, and babysitting the director's grandkids. I left after the busy Christmas season due to the constraints of my classes. But leaving was easier, honestly, because I'd stopped interacting with the people, the very thing I not only love to do but thrive on. I hate to be alone, and I hardly fit the definition of an introvert. I'd forgotten Jesus a little along the way too, and sometimes I wondered how life could be so good for some and not for others, even those who love him.

Then my godmother showed up. She's not my *official* godmother, but she renewed my life with Christ — and if that's not a godmother, I don't know what is. This woman gave me a passion for justice. She washed my feet and told me God wanted me to go work with the people no one else would go to, to touch the people no one else would touch. I took this as an undeniable call from God, a refreshing of what I already knew: If I didn't go work for the poor and unloved, I would be disobeying God and denying myself the very thing that fulfilled me in a way nothing else did.

That decision led me back to the CAC, doing laundry for people, running the store where we give out clothing and other household items, and trying to make some folks' gathering of their free, five-daily items into a nice shopping experience.

That's what is leading me to Swaziland with my mom. If I can bring just a little light to some people here in Lexington, maybe I can shine some of that in Africa. I don't think I'm going to change the world; maybe I'll just make someone's day. And I know it will change me. Despite my work at the CAC, I know I am sheltered and unaware of suffering on a grand scale. I need Africa more than it needs me.

Many people ask me why I want to go, and I never have a reason that doesn't sound totally weird. Talking about poverty and world-consciousness isn't a comfortable response. But I remember that Jesus was viewed as a weirdo too, so I say it anyway.

I simply know, like I know I'll wake up tomorrow, that going to Africa is part of what I'm meant to do. I'm meant to witness the pain and suffering and do my part to help. We're all part of the human family, and when one of us suffers, we all do. We need to do what we can to help one another. It is my hope that this trip to Africa will mark the beginning of my journey with God and a lifetime of working for justice.

It can be frustrating. Sometimes my friends talk about what they want to do with their lives—get a normal job, have a family, and maybe play a little golf or go to the lake on the weekend. Only then am I sad about the life I believe God has chosen for me. So many rich experiences will be mine, but I may miss out on a lot of normal life experiences for the typical American. I don't ever see myself joining a country club or living in a big house with two luxury cars. I'm OK with that most days. *Most* days.

I know it's going to be rough. Tom Davis, the president of Children's HopeChest—the ministry we're working with—says we are almost guaranteed to bawl at least half the trip home; that we'll have to fight everything in us to not take a child home. Imagine seeing all that suffering around you, he warned, and not being able to cure these children or their parents. What will it be like to hold a baby I know won't make it past the age of three or four? I guess all I can do for that child will be to hold her and give her the love she needs in that moment, for the beginning of her life is truly the end.

I'm going to try my best not to get emotionally attached, but that seems impossible right now. How can I *not* get emotionally attached to sweet, innocent children?

I'm not sure what I expect to find—I just know I have to go. I live such a privileged life that I can't even begin to imagine the life these people in Africa are living. I can't envision walking miles in the hot sun just to get a day's worth of food for our family. I can't imagine life in a small hut with no electricity or running water. I'm so used to my own cultural norms and values that it really is strange to step out of my own existence and try to see a life so different from my own. When I tell people about this trip, I act confident and excited. But I'm also scared. Not so much about what I will find there or what will happen to me physically, but what will happen to me emotionally. Looking at websites or commercials about starving and dying people is like staring at a painting. The painting may be intense and convicting, but I know I can turn away, slip on my soft pajamas, and curl up in my warm bed. After this trip, I won't be able to pretend these people aren't real. They will have names and faces. They will be just as real as my brother, Jake, my sister, Gwynnie, or my best friends.

I think this trip will be like having someone wake me up with a baseball bat.

❧❧❧❧

LISA

We're back home. And there's a bigger story to tell than simply the details of our trip to Swaziland. It's clear now that our journey began years before we ever thought of going to Africa. It took at least five years of upheaval and uncertainty for God's message—"To act justly and to love mercy and to walk humbly with your God" (Micah 6:8)—to take root in our family and begin to bear fruit. Seeds were planted in the hard soil of our hearts, and slowly, ever so slowly, shoots began to push toward the sky. Broken people came to us in various disguises—a young man kicked out of his home due to his sexual identity, a woman with missing teeth who brought stained toys for the kids and always appeared at the most inconvenient of times to have a chat, an addict who stole from us after we'd given him a job painting some rooms inside our house. We familiarized ourselves with the injustices in our state—Kentucky has many—and in our city, and joined an organization of churches seeking to provide better health care, transportation, and housing for those who struggle.

The fruit of five years of learning, longing, and leaning into the wind of the Spirit was this: we saw the need of our brothers and sisters in

Swaziland and took action—limited, flawed, sinful action, but action nonetheless.

Our trip to Swaziland isn't the whole story; it's a single chapter in the longer story of God snatching us out of our complacent, consumerist Christianity and flinging us into something more wonderful, wacky, liberal, and liberating.

The whole story is worth telling, because it might be your story too. If you're reading this at the airport on your way to Africa, feel free to skip to the second section. But if you're like us—uncomfortable about how comfortable you are and wondering if God has something to do with it—read on as we tell the story of how we learned to act justly, love mercy, and walk humbly with the God of all comfort and hope.

Come on over to The Third Street House, a slightly run-down Victorian we moved to a few years ago. Here we run what new monastics would call a "house of hospitality." If anyone needs a place to heal, ask questions, be safe, or just kick back for a bit, this is the place. Pull up a chair, and we'll share some of Ty's homemade ice cream with blueberries while you tell your story and we tell ours and we realize that we are all on this journey together.

So come on in, readers. Don't mind the dust. Will has a pot of homemade red sauce on the stove, and we'll have some pasta later; but for now, let's sit in the living room, and I'll tell you about our trip—the friends we made, the folks we met who minister in Swaziland, and some of the Swazi people who are making a difference in their homeland even as they suffer and die.

Make no mistake, suffering is assured for those who live in Swaziland—suffering of biblical proportions. Poverty, sickness, abuse, and oppression. This isn't a happy story, but it's worth telling. It's a story about suffering and hope, about death and life. It's a story about God-wrought transformations, beginning with our family. How did a family living in a five-thousand square-foot house in suburban Baltimore begin to care about justice, mercy, and the kingdom of God breaking in to our aching world?

Believe it or not, it all started with what seemed like a bad case of heartburn.

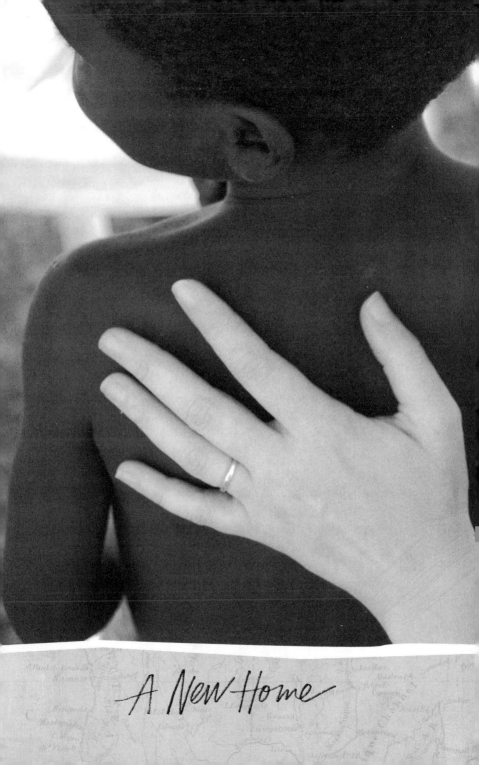

A New Home

1

〰〰〰

MEET MSSRS. WOLFF,
PARKINSON, AND WHITE

No wonder I had *heart*burn—my whole *body* should have been on fire, considering how much I was trying to do.

My mind-set matched with what many churchgoers feel these days: If serving God at church is a good thing, then volunteering at church for hours and hours a week must be even better. It might even make the Lord love me more!

Worship leader. Choir director. Sunday school teacher. Bulletin maker. Even baby-blanket-crocheting-ministry coordinator. I was wearing so many hats my head began to spin.

This was something more than simply seeking approval from those around me or feeling pressured to "use my gifts." Inside, I truly believed that God's affection for me was directly linked to how much I accomplished in his name—like how much I enjoy popcorn at the movies depends on how much fake butter the teenaged attendant squirts on. (Ask them to layer the butter next time you go.) My desire to please God was real enough, but it was formed by a need to know that God wasn't mad at me. I lived in fear that God might be rearing back in righteous indignation, or worse, disappointment—the kind of disappointment church had been reminding me of since day one (*Jesus loves me when I'm bad, even though it makes him sad*).

On a Sunday in March 2003, as we were driving home from another busy day at church, a burning pain beneath my lower rib cage made me white-knuckle the door handle of the car. The burning quickly increased from candle flame to blowtorch, and a gasp escaped my lips.

"What's wrong?" Will asked.

"I don't know." I gritted my teeth. "There's this burning in my abdomen."

A sensation of cold washed over the rest of my body, and I began to sweat profusely. I could hardly sit in my seat with the safety belt holding me in such burning agony. Nausea slammed my stomach.

"Do you want to go to the emergency room?" he asked.

"No. Just get me home."

When we pulled into the driveway, I shot out of the car and sprinted up the steps to our bathroom, ripping off my clothing along the way until, down to my underwear, I flung myself over the toilet bowl, retching and retching, sweat flowing down my forehead and in rivulets between my shoulder blades down my back. Afterward, I threw myself on the bed and curled in a fetal ball, rocking in agony.

Will still wanted to go to the emergency room.

Uh, no. "Just let me wait for an hour. If it's still like this, I'll go in." I only go to the hospital if something is bleeding or a baby needs to come out. Call it personal principle.

The attack lasted about a half hour, during which time I wondered if this was it, if I'd be going toward the light. As a person who deals with chronic depression, the thought wasn't terrifying. When I find a strange lump or bump, my first emotion is panic, then, "Meh."

I went to see my doctor the next day. The PA hooked me up to the ECG machine right there in the office. As the reading zigzagged across the paper, she examined the graph, then narrowed her eyes. "Hmm. This is odd. Let me hook you up again. There might be something wrong with those pads."

We went through a fresh set of pads, clippy clippy, and another round of that touchy metal arm drawing lines on new paper.

"Let me get Dr. Knight."

I love Dr. Knight. He doesn't act like he's so much smarter than I am.

He is, but still. It's not like he could write a novel. I appreciate people who know their boundaries in life.

As the PA peeled off the sheet of paper and headed out the door, I sat on the exam table wondering if I'd had a heart attack. I'd done my Internet research after the attack and been scared silly by *WebMD*. Judging by the symptoms I put into the search engine, I could have most definitely experienced one. A thirty-eight-year-old woman, three kids, a husband, a Volvo wagon, a big home in the Baltimore suburbs—I wasn't immune to nature's little sneak attacks. My maternal grandfather died of a heart attack at sixty-two. It was in the genes, right?

Dr. Knight needed only one look at the ECG results. "Have you ever been diagnosed with Wolff-Parkinson-White Syndrome?"

"No ..." I think I would have remembered that lovely sounding diagnosis.

He pointed out one line on the graph and said something about "strange rhythms," results typical for Wolff-Parkinson-White patients.

All I heard was *Parkinson*.

Dr. Knight must have seen my eyebrows shoot up because he quickly said, "It has nothing to do with Parkinson's disease!"

Phew.

Dr. Knight continued, "Now you're going to go home and look all this up on the Internet, and it's going to scare you silly—I know you better than to think you won't."

It's nice to have a doctor who knows me so well.

I went right home and discovered that I might have to have surgery and that there was a slight chance my heart could go into its funky quick step and I'd die. Right then and there, while reading *WebMD*.

And I had praise team practice to lead that night. Great. Just great.

2

⌀⌀⌀⌀

JUBILEE

After my visit to the cardiologist about two weeks after the attack, I was given the privilege of wearing a monitor around my neck like the world's tackiest piece of jewelry. I was told to press the Record button every time I felt my heart do its crazy dance, and each day I called in the recordings and heard my heart patterns as the sound transmitted over the phone line. Listening to those whirs and squeals, I knew I was going to die. Who can live with a heart that sounds like a cat in heat?

By the way, I didn't have a heart attack. I was almost disappointed. Think of how many people would have felt sorry for me! I could have milked those tidings for years and years. I'd never have to clean a toilet again, mow a lawn, or volunteer on "work day" at church. I could blame my heart for everything.

Wearing my beautiful institutional necklace, I headed over to my close friend Marty's for some one-on-one chat time. Marty and I can get sloppy with each other. We don't have to pretend we're perfect or that our lives are either. We were in the middle of coffee when Denise dropped by to show Marty some fabric for curtains Marty was creating for her house.

Denise was in the women's "care, share, and prayer" group Marty had started in her neighborhood. We began as a Bible study group, but we never did our homework and always ended up crying over our cares and woes, rejoicing over the good things, and praying together. We finally named ourselves "The Beth Moore Rejects." That fine lady would surely shake her head at our inability to buckle down and study the Word of God, but she'd probably cry with us at the kitchen table.

Denise rubbed me the wrong way when I first met her. She firmly declared that free will was what the Bible taught. I was a five-point Calvinist at the time, and nobody tells *us* what the Bible teaches. Reformed folk are the smarty-pants Protestants of Christendom—the educated, the well-reasoned, the defenders of the faith once delivered unto the saints. We know what's in the Bible, baby, and it all starts with God's T.U.L.I.P.

When Denise saw me on Marty's couch, her eyes lit up. "I can't believe you're here!" she said, digging into her purse and pulling out her Bible. "I was just praying through Scripture for you last night, and God showed me these verses and I wrote them down."

As Denise was praying the night before, she told me, some words from God had come to her as well. I don't know if you believe stuff like this can happen. I used to be highly skeptical of people hearing from God personally. I mean, *sola scriptura* and all of that. (I'm not sure if any Christian *really* believes that the only God-inspired thoughts come directly from the Bible, thank heavens.) Denise handed me a slip of paper with words that are chiseled into my heart forever.

God knows you're doing good works to please him, but he wants your heart.

Wants my *heart*? I gave him my heart when I was three, didn't I? I distinctly remember climbing onto my mother's bed, hearing her words about my sin and needing a savior and did I want to ask Jesus into my heart? I certainly did! Jesus healed people and stuck up for the nice guys. And he made a lot of food from a very little bit. That was neat! I read those Arch Books, and I knew exactly who Jesus was.

As I grew up, I went forward in my Christian school at times to rededicate my life to Christ. We had a retreat each fall at a big campground, and I dedicated myself again, and again resolved not to listen to my rock 'n roll records. I threw out *The Grand Illusion* by Styx at least three times. Then I took my show on the road, graduating from a Christian university, for cryin' out loud!

I married a Christian man, was raising Christian kids, and was serving like crazy at church. I was even teaching Sunday school, which I'm not very good at, which probably counted for more with God because I was so miserable doing it.

And God was questioning whether I'd given him my heart? Please!

But my doubt only lasted about three seconds. Everybody needs a prophet—someone who cuts through the noise and tells it like it is—and I began to consider whether Denise might be mine.

I left Marty's house soon afterward, the slip of paper in my purse. As I drove away from Marty's street, I heard the words, "Drive. Just drive. You'll know what I want you to see when you get there."

The words weren't audible, by the way. If this Holy Spirit communication thing really is a delusion, at least I'm not hearing audible voices. I'm not that far gone.

So I pulled out of Marty's neighborhood on that morning in April and headed south on some of Harford County's older roads. I crossed over a couple of the aging iron bridges and drove past immaculately preserved estates until I entered Baltimore County and turned onto Jericho Road. I didn't get the significance of the road's name at the time, but my walls were about to come tumbling down—and if I'd known then where I'd be now, I think I would have driven home and turned on the television.

Along the Gunpowder River, a gracious house from the 1700s sits about thirty feet from the banks. It rests sideways on the lot, its stone walls whitewashed. I've always loved that house. When it went up for sale a few years before, I checked the price just in case. This day as I drove slowly past it, a white oval sign hung down, its simple script telling the name of the house.

Jubilee.

"Jubilee. That's it. That's your word." The words rung in my head.

Jubilee. It made sense. The word had come into my conversation several times in the past week. I headed for home, picked up my Bible, and began reading about the Year of Jubilee God wanted Israel to celebrate every fifty years. (Not that they ever did, but that's a different story.)

My husband was in for a surprise when he got home.

❧❧❧

God knows you're doing good works to please him, but he wants your heart.

Do those words resonate with you?

This book may be different from others you've read about social justice. But let's be honest with each other, since we're sitting here together on my sofa at The Third Street House. (Can I get you a cup of tea, by the way?)

Everything I'm about to tell you about social justice boils down to this: God wants your heart. That may seem like another point entirely, but I believe this single simple truth will help you bathe in the deep waters of justice instead of dipping your toes in now and again.

One of my favorite passages of Scripture is 1 John chapter four because it tells us that *love* is what this Christian life is all about—God loving each of his children, and us loving God and others in return.

> Dear friends, let us love one another, for love comes from God. Everyone who loves has been born of God and knows God. Whoever does not love does not know God, because God is love. This is how God showed his love among us: He sent his one and only Son into the world that we might live through him. This is love: not that we loved God, but that he loved us and sent his Son as an atoning sacrifice for our sins. Dear friends, since God so loved us, we also ought to love one another. No one has ever seen God; but if we love one another, God lives in us and his love is made complete in us.
>
> 1 John 4:7–12

One of the hardest things for me to accept was the fact that God loves me *period*, not that God loves me *if.* I viewed life as if what I was doing *had* to count—why do something if it doesn't count? God the Father may have taken me on, but only because I believed in Jesus; God most likely didn't care for me, Lisa Marie, all that much. Surely he was sick and tired of my prayers of need, my depression, my temper, my laziness. God loved me the way I loved the gripers and complainers at church—grudgingly and with conditions.

"God is love," writes John.

In my Christian life I hear these words a lot: "God is love. But God is also just."

Yes, God is just; but God is not justice. It's important to make the distinction in the parts of speech. *Love* is a noun. *Just* is an adjective. We don't say, "God is love, and God is justice." God's justice—his way of acting justly—always flows from his essential nature, his character. God *is* love—because God cannot *not* love. God cannot choose to turn off his love without destroying a part of himself. Love is the state of God's being; God, as a being, is love.

I don't pretend to be a theologian, but I sleep better at night believing this of my Father in heaven with my whole heart.

Tucked in the folds of God's love like a handwritten note in a jacket pocket is this beautiful truth: God delights in his children (Psalm 147:11). Delight is something that flows from the heart of God when he looks at his wayward children. God's love generates delight, inescapably, as sunlight cannot help but call out the colors of a garden.

I have a friend to whom bad things happen again and again. Just when things are looking up, something falls apart; and yet she has the greatest faith in God I've ever seen. Faith for her daily bread, the lights, her clothes. This is what she says about God: "I always think God is just a great big old lovebug."

If we believe God delights in us, that God cannot *not* love us, we find trust easier to come by and harder to lose. We understand there will always be enough in the economy of love, and that we can share all we have because God will never leave us or forsake us. People who know God loves them know he will provide. They have put him to the test, and he comes through every time.

People who know God loves them know he loves everyone else too. Believing that makes all the difference if you decide to live your life for others, as Jesus did.

If you're a parent, remember when your child was born and your heart felt like it was going to burst out of your chest and throat and eyes all at once?

God loves you like that.

If you've ever been in love, remember how your lover is the first thing on your mind when you wake up, the focus of your entire day, and the final, fair dream in your heart as you go to sleep?

God loves you like that.

The story of how I learned that truth—and learned to remember it every day—is a long one. Let's grab some of Ty's homemade bread and keep talking.

3

JUBILEE, OH JUBILEE

I grew up in the Christian school movement of the seventies and eighties. We memorized Scripture, learned our ABCs, the Ten Commandments, Psalms 23 and 100, and had chapel every Friday morning. Sometimes the teachers and staff would work up a musical number. One trio in particular consisted of the school secretary and two ladies from the church that sponsored my school. They sang "That Happy Jubilee" at least once a year.

Praise the Lord I've been invited
to a meeting in the air,
in Jubilee, Jubilee.
All the saints of all the ages
in their glory will be there,
Oh, I'm going to that happy Jubilee!
With that glorious assembly
dressed in garments pure and white,
in Jubilee, Jubilee.
You will find me for I'm watching
and my lamp is trimmed and bright,
Oh, I'm going to that happy Jubilee!

I always pictured Jubilee like a big party—everybody in comfy, soft white robes laughing together, finally at rest from the wars and strife of life on earth. It would be like the biggest birthday bash ever. And I couldn't wait.

But what did it mean now? Why had God brought a middle-aged woman with a faulty heart out into the countryside to read the word *Jubilee* on the side of a stately house?

As I read in the Bible (and then read it again just to make sure) about what the Jubilee Year consisted of—giving the land a much-needed rest, all debts being forgiven, and so much more—I knew I was being asked to put away my writing for a year. Of course, Will had just taken a job that paid about two-thirds the salary of his old one. But his office was closer to home, and we'd see him more—a priceless arrangement, to be sure!

It might seem that I should have agonized over this for days before telling him. But I didn't. The words of Scripture hit my brain as if someone were yelling them through a megaphone. I did feel a little warm and shaky as I read, and I wondered how it would work, but, like taking your child to kindergarten or preparing supper for the family, this wasn't optional. I knew without a doubt, and right away, that God was speaking to me. My heart, due to his grace, recognized his voice.

But it was going to take some faith. We still had the big house, the cars, and the private school to pay for. I was taking a sort of Jubilee, but the surrounding features of my life didn't change. I knew things might have to change, but how, and when?

I waited for a big word from God as I tried to give him my heart—even though I still wasn't sure what that meant. I planned to do a "big-time" Bible reading plan. Long story short, I didn't. All I could handle were the Gospels, reading about Jesus over and over. A spiritual journal? That didn't happen either. What I did with my days during those first few months, I couldn't really tell you. Somehow I managed to do little other than the usual church and family responsibilities. I think I played a lot of Text Twist and Shape Shifter as well.

And somehow our bills were being paid on time, although my regular trips to T.J. Maxx had been somewhat curtailed!

Still nothing. No big insight from God. No fireworks of love exploding in my heart. I *wanted* to want to love God with all of me, but I felt like I'd been stranded in the desert with a shovel and told to find water.

Spring faded into summer. I took my kids to swim at my sister's pool. We ate crabs and read books. And I still waited.

Then something happened. In August, we attended a faith and arts festival in England called Greenbelt. I was severely jet-lagged and sleeping in a teepee, of all things. Meanwhile, as I slept away the festival evenings, Will was busy chatting it up. My guy is a first-class networker. At big events, I'm the one stapled to the carpet near the steamed shrimp, calculating when I can politely return to the bathroom to hide out for ten or fifteen minutes.

Will hung out in the pub at night and talked with a couple from Lexington, Kentucky, who were involved in something called "intentional Christian community." I had to have Will explain it to me at least three times before I began to understand.

Community. Caring for each other to care for the other. But who is "the other"?

The answer to that question caused my boat to rock side to side and front to back so hard that only Jesus kept me inside. Jesus, whom I'd been reading about over and over during my time of Jubilee—my time of Jubilee when I stopped letting myself say "but" to all of his hard sayings.

> Then he will say to those on his left, "Depart from me, you who are cursed, into the eternal fire prepared for the devil and his angels. For I was hungry and you gave me nothing to eat, I was thirsty and you gave me nothing to drink, I was a stranger and you did not invite me in, I needed clothes and you did not clothe me, I was sick and in prison and you did not look after me."
>
> Matthew 25:41–43

C'mon, Jesus, salvation is by grace alone through faith alone. You can pray a prayer and be done with it. What's all this business about what I did and didn't do? Hasn't Jesus read Saint Paul?

And what about the story of the rich young ruler? Jesus *couldn't* have been serious, could he? I mean, the poor fellow comes to this dynamic teacher everybody's been talking about and gets shut down. You'd have thought Jesus would have bent over backward to make the guy comfy. After all, with Judas nipping regularly from their purse, I'm sure the wandering band of disciples could have used the money. "What must I do to inherit eternal life?" the influential young man asks (Luke 18:18).

"Sell all your goods to feed the poor."

He did *not* just say that!

The young ruler went away sad. I would have too. I mean, Jesus *had* to have meant something else. He was using hyperbole — it says so right here in the notes of my study Bible!

"How hard it is for the rich to enter the kingdom of God," Jesus told his disciples upon the gentleman's departure.

And then there's the passage about leaving your brother and sister, mother and father, letting the dead bury the dead, and following Jesus (Luke 9:57 – 62). What does that even mean? Wouldn't that make some of the people you're leaving really mad? Wouldn't it hurt the others?

Trying to work through the words of Jesus was almost like struggling with a really gnarly sin. I couldn't find a safe place to discuss it. So many of my Christian friends became touchy, and I don't blame them. When you're contemplating such difficult teachings, you can come down hard on the church, yourself, other Christians — pretty much everyone with a pulse. Talking about living like Jesus did is dangerous and divisive. At least Will and I stood on similar ground by this time. He was miles ahead of me for months, talking about "marginalized people" and "If our congregations interpret the gospel for the world, what are we saying?" He was beginning to hang out with people with crazy hair and clothes (but cool glasses) who obviously felt there wasn't a question that wasn't worth asking. I felt a cloying resentment. Was he becoming a liberal? A radical? A *bad* Christian? Jesus couldn't really be *followed*, could he? I was supposed to *believe* in him, sure, but *follow*? Nobody really expected any of us to do *that*, did they?

In the name of grace (a wonderful thing to be sure), I'd watered down faith to mere intellectual assent. I didn't have to follow Jesus, really — I had only to believe he was the Son of God and go on my merry way. Believing correctly was one more thing to check off my to-do list. But Jesus didn't talk like that. Not even close. Nor did James, who wrote, "Even the demons believe ... and shudder" (James 2:19).

Was God really calling me to be conformed to the image of his Son? Wasn't it more like a suggestion? What if I just wanted to make sure I went to heaven and not hell? What if I simply valued church for the fellowship, the children's programs, and the potlucks?

Was God talking about *actually changing* my life? Really?

No wonder the Pharisees hated Jesus. No wonder the rich man went away sad.

Not only that, this "intentional community" business was taking over my husband. He was always talking about how our communities can shape our world and bring about the kingdom. Wouldn't it be great to try something like that? I said—"when hell freezes over."

Don't go checking down there, but I think there's a bit of a cold spot somewhere.

This weird community he was so enamored with fed the poor, helped resettle refugees, counseled addicts, and even went so far as to wear fair trade clothing! Now that was going just a little too far.

They moved to downtown Lexington to live in closer proximity to the poor and marginalized. They had amazing stories, I had to admit, but I could live my life without tales about dragging homeless people off the street during a cold snap—I'd done it just fine for forty years, thank you very much.

I didn't have to ask questions about who was near to the heart of God and come up with any other answer than myself, my family, and my friends, did I? I wasn't being invited to ask what God was doing in the world and how I could play a part, was I?

That stuff was for radicals, not regular women like me.

It was then I began to feel stalked by God.

Soon Mr. Community had us all on a plane to Glorieta, New Mexico, for something called "The Emergent Gathering," a meeting of all those people who helped him question the church and sometimes helped me question his salvation! OK, that's hyperbole, but he sure did make me question his commitment to "defending the faith once delivered to the saints," I can tell you that!

We had a growing list of urgent questions. What does it really mean to be the people of God? How can a family of five follow God in the way of Jesus? What is God really doing in the world? What is true Christianity? And will everyone we meet be so freaky? (OK, that was my question alone.)

At first, the folks gathered in Glorieta didn't set us entirely at ease. There was more simple living, more radical talk about poverty and service and redeeming food from dumpsters. Completely unsure of where all this was leading, I decided to pull a Gideon, which is a nice way of saying I let out my inner brat.

The second day, I took the kids to the local Gas 'n Sip. We bought some of the junkiest junk food we could find: Guacamole Doritos, marshmallows, squirt cheese, Ritz crackers, Slim Jims, and pink Canada Dry ginger ale. The more nitrates and preservatives the better! We wanted to see if these people would still accept us after seeing what we bought, or if they were really running some kind of club for cool Christians who were tired of "church as usual." Driving back, we imagined all the terrible reactions and judgments that were going to be thrown our way.

As soon as we walked through the door, we scattered our bad-on-so-many-levels loot on the island in the kitchen like kids coming home from a Halloween haul for the record books. Then we stepped back.

Guess what? Everyone loved it.

Before long, we were quizzing each other about our favorite junk foods while washing down Easy Cheese with glowing soda.

We began to feel at ease around these people, and—maybe we weren't so different after all—maybe we were united by something more important than our clothing or our hairstyles.

It was after the junk-food junket that we met a wonderful couple, Geoff and Sherry, and learned they lived in Lexington, Kentucky, where they'd started an intentional Christian community in the late nineties. Really?

Yep, Lexington. The same community we had learned about. In England.

God was up to something, and he wasn't exactly being obscure about it.

Honestly, I love it when he does that. Only not when it involves changing my life completely.

4

DENISE THE PROPHETESS
SHOWS UP AGAIN

Throughout autumn and winter and into early 2004, I was twisted up inside about what God wanted from me—why in the world would God be so crazy as to ask me to move to the inner city, to take my children there, to get us all raped and pillaged and murdered for the sake of the kingdom. Will thought it sounded great. Intentional Christian community downtown—heigh-ho!

Heigh-NO!

For years I'd criticized missionaries who left their young child at some boarding school to be raised by teachers so they could preach the gospel instead of parent. And now this? No way.

I didn't just say no to Will. I told God *he'd* gone too far too. I know Jesus said, "Deny yourself, take up your cross, and follow me," but there wasn't even a Lexington, Kentucky, in existence when he uttered those words. "This, my Friend," I said to God, "is a loophole, and I've just jumped through it."

Jesus tapped his foot.

OK, maybe intentional Christian community, but *not* downtown. We could find a modest little house in what our family calls the "urbs," not too far from downtown. Nothing glitzy, maybe a post-war neighborhood with little saltboxes and ranchers on quarter-acre lots. We could pile in our station wagon, drive downtown to serve people in need, go to our fellowship gatherings, then head back home to our safe spot where the people we ministered to wouldn't hold us up, ask us for money, or sleep on our porch. That sounded more normal; that would be fine. (I wasn't considering the fact that you're more likely to die from an auto accident in the suburbs than you are to be murdered in the city.)

One night during this time of questioning, the phone rang at 10:00 p.m. When I heard Denise's voice, I was excited. I've always been thankful God chooses to communicate with me so extravagantly, and I knew I was in a real pickle about all these possible changes. Jubilee was one thing; Kentucky another thing entirely.

Gwynnie, our youngest daughter, had been lying low with migraines, poor thing, at least four times a week — doubled over in bed, rocking, throwing up, head throbbing in intense pain. She'd had migraines since she was five, but they'd increased in number and intensity. The Rejects were praying. I was more than a little concerned, as you might surmise, wondering if a tumor had taken over her brain.

Denise said, "I just had to call you with these Scriptures. I was praying about Gwynnie, and God kept giving me these passages. I'm not sure what they really have to do with Gwynnie, but here they are."

I slid a pencil and a scrap of paper off my nightstand. Jotting down the references, I listened as she also told me she thought God wanted me to fast. "Sundown to sundown," she said. "The old Jewish way. In solitude if you can."

Interestingly enough, I'd been getting the fasting message too while agonizing in prayer over my daughter. I didn't *want* that to be the message because I'm the worst faster in the world. I don't get that spiritual high, I still forget to pray as much as I should, and suddenly all the good food seems to show itself. "That affirms what I've been hearing," I said.

So I called my girlfriend Leigh, who has a guest suite in her home. I could shut myself in the bedroom; the bathroom was right off the bedroom, with no access to the hallway. Perfect.

I holed myself up in the room as the sun heaved its last purple breath outside the window, laid down on the bed, and waited for God to speak. *Hmm.*

It was dark, finally. The sun had set, the fasting had begun, so what's next, God? I'm here. I showed up.

I tried to still my breathing. I prayed. I sought to clear my mind from the normal worries of life, to become centered (whatever that means) and peaceful.

Can I confess something? I'm the worst contemplative in the history of Christendom. While I'm trying to concentrate on Jesus, my NASCAR mind speeds along, remembering I forgot to pay the cable bill and considering that I'd better use that ground beef in the fridge by tomorrow or I'll have to throw it out. And why do schools need immunization records anyway? Don't they know how hard it is to gather all that if you've moved around as much as we have?

Finally, I sat up and grabbed my Bible. I picked up the scrap of paper with Denise's verses and hoped God would speak through the passages, because he sure wasn't speaking through the static of my brain.

I turned to Isaiah 58:1 – 12. I realize this is a long passage of Scripture to reproduce in a book, but it changed my life completely. I mean that literally. I am a totally different person today, five years later, because I read Isaiah 58 that night. (If you're the daring sort, pray before you read it that God would speak to you too.)

> "Shout it aloud, do not hold back.
>> Raise your voice like a trumpet.
> Declare to my people their rebellion
>> and to the house of Jacob their sins.
> For day after day they seek me out;
>> they seem eager to know my ways,
> as if they were a nation that does what is right
>> and has not forsaken the commands of its God.
> They ask me for just decisions
>> and seem eager for God to come near them.
> 'Why have we fasted' they say,
>> 'and you have not seen it?
> Why have we humbled ourselves,

and you have not noticed?'

"Yet on the day of your fasting, you do as you please
    and exploit all your workers.
Your fasting ends in quarreling and strife,
    and in striking each other with wicked fists.
You cannot fast as you do today
    and expect your voice to be heard on high.
Is this the kind of fast I have chosen,
    only a day for a man to humble himself?
Is it only for bowing one's head like a reed
    and for lying on sackcloth and ashes?
Is that what you call a fast,
    a day acceptable to the Lord?

"Is not this the kind of fasting I have chosen:
to loose the chains of injustice
    and untie the cords of the yoke,
to set the oppressed free
    and break every yoke?
Is it not to share your food with the hungry
    and to provide the poor wanderer with shelter—
when you see the naked, to clothe him,
    and not to turn away from your own flesh and blood?
Then your light will break forth like the dawn,
    and your healing will quickly appear;
then your righteousness will go before you,
    and the glory of the Lord will be your rear guard.
Then you will call, and the Lord will answer;
    you will cry for help, and he will say: Here am I.

"If you do away with the yoke of oppression,
    with the pointing finger and malicious talk,
and if you spend yourselves in behalf of the hungry
    and satisfy the needs of the oppressed,
then your light will rise in the darkness,

and your night will become like the noonday.
The LORD will guide you always;
    he will satisfy your needs in a sun-scorched land
    and will strengthen your frame.
You will be like a well-watered garden,
    like a spring whose waters never fail.
Your people will rebuild the ancient ruins
    and will raise up the age-old foundations;
you will be called Repairer of Broken Walls,
    Restorer of Streets with Dwellings."

In a friend's guest room, as I sat in the pool of light from the lamp on the nightstand, God talked to me.

Was I spending myself in behalf of the poor and the oppressed? I could talk about the need to reach out until the porch light went on. I was great at criticizing church people for not getting their hands and feet dirty. But was I really doing anything to help the poor and needy, the lonely, the sick, the prisoner?

Nope.

All the promises God lavishes on those who do those things — oh, wow! To be a Repairer of Broken Walls and Restorer of Streets with Dwellings, that's what *righteous* means? That's *what God wants* from his people?

More verses flowed beneath my gaze as I read down the list, each passage convincing me further that God was leading us in a new direction, a different path that would guide our feet to people he cared about, to people who needed to know that Jesus cared about them hour after day after week.

I was called to be his hands. His feet. Act justly, love mercy, walk humbly.

But wait — one more thing — the biggest thing: *What about my kids, Lord? Remember them? The people who would be in danger every day if we moved?*

I turned to the final verse on Denise's list: Deuteronomy 1:39: "And the little ones that you said would be taken captive, your children who do not yet know good from bad—they will enter the land. I will give it to them and they will take possession of it."

Suddenly I realized I was having a real conversation with God. As a family we'd been praying the story of Abraham since Advent. We wanted to go to the land the Lord had prepared for us. God had just given me the green light that all would be well. Talking to God this way was thrilling, but a little freaky too!

If this was God's will, so be it.

I emerged the next morning and told my friend, "We're moving to the city." I still wasn't totally sure it was Lexington. We hadn't visited yet. It could have been Baltimore City. I didn't know. But I was ready for the adventure. Furthermore, leaving behind our comfortable life was a choice I was ready to make.

It's not like I would have to give up my shiny Volvo. Right?

5

⟋⟍⟋⟍

FREAKY FRIDAY

Before heading down to visit Lexington for the first time, we spent a weekend with The Simple Way folks in Philadelphia. One of the founders, Shane Claiborne, has become a folk hero of sorts for his commitment to the poor, and he's also one of the nicest people you'll ever meet. My kids love him.

In late February, we pulled our Volvo wagon up to an old, run-down church. We looked ultra-suburbanite, and the car didn't help either. Let me tell you a little bit about that car. At that time, I drove a Volvo V70 Turbo wagon, a silver bullet of a car. It was my dream "mom" car. Behind the wheel, I felt superior and classy and usually way more fabulous than anyone else in the after-school carpool lane. It also beat most other cars off the line when the light turned green. Baby, when that turbo kicked in — *mm, mmm!* I was Queen of the Blacktop.

After parking that car, locking it, turning on the security system, double-checking if it was locked, and rearming the security system, we walked inside the church. I looked around me and — how shall I say this? — I freaked out.

What was God playing at? Did I have to have dreadlocks? Did I have to wear oddly made, hand-sewn clothing? Did I have to be a vegetarian? The only thing that makes me happier than cheeseburgers is a rib-eye steak! Did I have to ride a bike everywhere and wear strange glasses? (I could still keep my Mac and my cell phone, apparently, since a lot of people had those.)

I felt about as comfortable as a ten-foot woman in a Mini Cooper. Wearing paper underwear. And vinyl shoes two sizes too small. I wasn't wearing a long, home-knit scarf, and I clearly wasn't genetically capable of putting an outfit together with Che Guevara hats and fatigue jackets constructed from animal-free components. I liked lipstick and cute sandals, for goodness' sake! Was God calling me to love him and serve the poor, or to join a club of impoverished, hipster Jesus freaks?

I wanted out before I was in. I appreciated what these folks were doing, don't get me wrong, but there was no way I'd ever fit in. I didn't know if I'd ever be accepted with my little Christian novels, my Old Navy jeans, and three blonde children. I'd never been arrested for nonviolent civil disobedience—and never wanted to—and back then, I figured the School of the Americas was a sister campus to American University.

The food seemed a tad creepy too—odd veggies I'd barely heard of, curries, soups, and stews. I wondered how long it had been since anyone there had eaten a box of Kraft macaroni and cheese or a plump greasy chicken leg from KFC—with the skin on, I might add.

In short, they were odd, and I was old. Old old old. (I *did* have a tattoo, so maybe that counted for something.)

It's frustrating when my biases make me interpret people and situations with such error. I imagined sinister glances from every side, but was that really what was happening? Mr. Social, of course, was having the time of his life. I hoped and prayed that Philly wasn't the city Will and I were being called to, because if it was, I was bailing out. I gave God a choice: Find another city or get another girl.

The kids were miserable. The church had almost no heat, and, as is common for this movement, there's little activity planned for older children. Toddlers and young children, yes. After all, most of the people involved in new monasticism are young. Ty, Jake, and Gwynnie sat on the hard pew and were hardly of a mind to appreciate what was going on up front—people reporting in from their various communities, telling how God was moving and community was forming.

Scheduled to stay the night in a community house nearby, I put my foot down. "I'm driving the kids back to Baltimore tonight and sleeping there, and I'll come back by myself tomorrow."

I was never so glad to sleep in my own bed. Not only that, we were so programmed for "programs" I never thought there'd be nothing for *my* children.

The next day, I arrived back at the church early in the morning, with my sleeping bag. And I sat back down next to Will—who had, naturally, had a great time the night before—and hunkered down into the downy warmth.

I wish I could tell you I enjoyed the day, and there were times I let down my guard—around the lunch table, or when we sang. But when we slid back into the car, I was glad to go. I'd never felt more uncomfortable in my life, fully aware at the time that God doesn't usually call us to comfort.

I think God was having a little fun with me by using my early experiences of Christian community to say, "See? It could be worse. Trust me." I realized this when we arrived a week later in Lexington to *communality* (the name of this community of faith and action), entered the home of Geoff and Sherry, whom we'd met in New Mexico, and it felt *normal*. Geoff, being a native Australian, served great tea and cookies with sugar, which put me immediately at ease. When I asked Geoff if he was a vegetarian, he said, "I don't believe I'm capable of turning down a steak."

I think I heard the "Hallelujah Chorus."

I am amazed by how spoiled I am. God could have called us to Philly, but he didn't, so I didn't have to say "no thanks." God knew what I was capable of at that point. I love that about God. At times I feel ashamed of my own softness. I was too soft to bear a cold church building, too proud to mingle with people—my brothers and sisters in Christ!—who looked and acted differently. All I could pray was, *God help me.*

And he did.

And he does.

6

⟨≈≈⟩

GOOSEBUMPS

During our visit with the members of *communality*, we decided to look at houses. I finally knew in my heart what Will had known for months: we were being called to live in Lexington in intentional community, and it sure beat suffering in Philly! Sherry, a beautiful, brown-eyed woman with a yoga body and expressive hands, drove Ty and me through neighborhood after neighborhood. Not much was for sale in the areas we preferred. Later, she made us tea, and we sat in her tidy, terra-cotta-colored kitchen.

"Now, I almost don't want to tell you this because I don't want to put any pressure on you, but there's this house ..." She swiped her dark curls away from her face, picked up her mug with both hands, and took a sip.

"Oh yeah?"

"Well, this friend of the community bought it several years ago, and we did a lot of work on the place to fix it up. Some community members live there now, and we've done ministry from there, but it's just become financially unfeasible for us to keep it going. So the owner is going to sell it. He hasn't put it on the market yet" — she placed her strong hand on my arm and squeezed — "but don't feel obligated or anything. I just thought you might like to see it."

"Of course."

"And really, we've prayed about it and we're letting it go, so we're fine with whatever happens to the house."

I found out later that *communality* had put multiple hundreds of volunteer hours into that old house.

I headed over with Sherry and Ty to check it out—*whoa.*

It was a rambling Victorian on Third Street with tons of windows and thirteen-foot ceilings downstairs. It had a cool apartment in the attic, and the living room was deep red, just like my kitchen back home. There was still a lot of work left to be done, but it was definitely in livable condition. Built in 1882, it had good bones and some fine woodworking, and it was quirky.

I love quirky.

Will inspected it next. We talked with the owner and discussed the work that had been done and what was left to do. We walked the long, creaking staircase and stood in the rooms, imagining what life would be like in a home so different from our previous one. "We'll let you know," we told the owner, "as soon as we decide."

On our way out of town that night, I asked Sherry to draw us a map to The Third Street House and then to the highway back east toward Maryland. As she drew, she inked a little square on Third Street and wrote a number.

I pointed to it and said, "What's that?"

"Oh, that's the house number."

I sucked in my breath as I held up the sheet to Will and Ty. "Look at the house number."

Their jaws dropped open, and I swear my mother was watching us from heaven at the moment and probably laughing out loud. I heard Mom say, "It's OK with me. I'm behind this."

"What?" Geoff asked, noticing our stunned expressions.

"That's our *current* house number," I said. "The house my mom built, our house in Maryland."

The house I never thought I could leave.

If God had sent down a singing angel it wouldn't have been more clear.

We were moving to Lexington.

On May 30, 2005, we packed ourselves and our yowling cats into our Volvos (Ty has an old Volvo beater) and drove to Lexington. We were ready to live a different life in a different town. We'd finally said yes.

It was the same Jesus, though. He was just asking us to follow him, further up and further in.

I didn't know then, thank God, how lonely, frustrating, and sad the next two years would be—how I'd come to feel in my bones the truth of Jesus' declaration, "I did not come to bring peace, but a sword," turning son against father, daughter against mother (Matthew 10:34–35).

I couldn't blame everyone else for thinking we were crazy—that's what I thought too. But Jesus was clear: we didn't have a choice. Unless you count ignoring his call a choice.

Our family didn't. Life doesn't last forever.

7

❧

MOUNTAINTOP REMOVAL, FOUR BLONDE CHILDREN, AND A SURLY COOK

One of my favorite memories is two-year-old Ty singing "A Whole New World" from the Disney movie *Aladdin*. She'd paste an earnest look on her face and sing it with such emotion that we'd bust out laughing.

Not long after we moved to Lexington, I realized I was in a whole new world—and not the G-rated animated kind either. Faster than a metroliner, introductions to new people and causes and issues hurtled my way—refugees escaping war and famine and coming to America, human trafficking, environmental racism, food access issues, mountaintop removal.

Mountaintop what?

Either my new friends were crazy, or the Christianity I'd grown up with had had its head in the ground, the clouds, or both.

My ignorance of these things didn't make them less real—or less of a problem. I learned that mountaintop removal consists of dynamiting the tops of mountains in Appalachia in order to get at the coal seams beneath, and then the waste rock is piled in the valleys below. More than 1,200 miles of streams have been covered up in Appalachia, and over 500 mountains have been blasted to smithereens. Flooding occurs, animals are killed, clean water is polluted, people can't bathe their children or drink their water, asthma is rampant—and mountaintop removal provides no new jobs or useful benefits. Drug use has spread like the flu.

I'm supposed to care about this?

Yes, Lisa. Read Isaiah 58 again.

A group of students from state colleges had come to Lexington that summer to raise awareness about the mountaintop removal going on east of us. They called the happenings Mountain Justice Summer, and they were using High Street House—the place out of which our community ministers and in which it gathers for Sunday fellowship and Wednesday group—as a sort of headquarters and rest stop between events.

"I bet they'd love some watermelon," I thought on a sweltering afternoon soon after the group's arrival, and cut one up into thick, cold slices—two large bowls piled high with red, sweet fruit. I and the kids, now eight, eleven, and fifteen, carried the watermelon over to High Street where twenty-five or thirty people were hanging out. The guys on the steps were friendly, greeting me and the kids and gratefully accepting wedges of watermelon.

Inside, however, I was met with distrustful looks. I suppose I *did* look odd. We were on our way to the pool, and I had on a hot-pink wrap over my zebra print bathing suit, and my hair was twisted up in a clippie. Can you say *suburban housewife*? Counting our friend Abbey, I had four blonde children in tow. Not one young woman smiled or even nodded at me. Talk about having cold water thrown on my fire of helpfulness. If Christian activists were weirder than me, it seemed that secular activists were just as weird and not nearly as nice.

Of course, part of me thought, "Well, girls, thanks for judging me and dismissing me without knowing who I am or where my journey is taking me."

And then part of me realized that I was judging and dismissing *them* without knowing who they were or where their journey was taking them and their hairy legs and armpits. (Ouch, I did it again!) *God, help me.*

And he did.

And he does.

I'm discovering that following Jesus isn't just walking the path but reminding myself again and again that the path exists at all. God doesn't ask us to judge whether someone is worthy to receive antiretrovirals (ARVs) for AIDS, or watermelon, for that matter. He calls us to help.

During this time, as we met refugees as well, I realized there's a big world out there that Jesus died for and loves too. A seed for Swaziland was planted then, I suppose, in the knowing that Jesus meant what he said in John 3:16 — most likely the first Bible verse I'd ever memorized — that God loves the world.

About three months later, I began volunteering at the Catholic Action Center (CAC), a white-brick cube that houses a soup kitchen, showers, a phone, and a large rec room where folks can sleep when the weather dips below freezing. I don't know about you, but I wouldn't want to be on the street when the thermometer reads thirty-one degrees. I can barely stand my sixty-degree house in the winter. (We have to keep the thermometer that low to afford the utility bills — shades of that church in Philly, right?)

I'd been given various tasks in the kitchen at the CAC, working all the while under the distrustful eye of Jacob the cook. Why didn't he trust me — this woman who appeared out of nowhere, drove a fancy Volvo, and hummed while she filled the utility sink with scalding water to soak the begrimed burner grates from the industrial range?

His silence bothered me.

I was a cheerleader in high school. I was used to people liking me and thinking I was G-R-E-A-T! I wasn't the snobby kind of cheerleader, either: I had friends *two* years younger than me. I was the Senior Sweetheart, for crying out loud! How in the world could Jacob just ignore me or reply in grunts and monosyllables?

I scrubbed, scrubbed, scrubbed, and I sliced, sliced, sliced four mornings a week, Jacob keeping a watchful eye as I became, what I realize now, an apprentice. And isn't that just the way? I figured I was coming to help, to make things better, to be the savior of the kitchen. I chattered nervously at times. "My daughter loves potatoes," or "Ugh! Do you think I can salvage anything from this broccoli?" But I was learning so much more.

It took a carton of rotten tomatoes for Jacob to reach back toward me in my old jeans and a bandana — toward this woman who needed more from him than he'd ever need from me. The tomatoes hadn't rotted all the way through, so I sliced away the black spots, the watery bruises, and the fuzz. In my own kitchen, I wouldn't have been able to do that without gagging, but God gave me grace for the task. I sliced and diced the bad bits out of every last tomato and put the good sections on the stove to simmer, along with six bags of spinach and five pounds of potatoes, hoping it would make a nice base for Jacob to work with.

When I went home that day, I left a big bowl of chopped potatoes beside a smaller bowl of sliced onions, since Jacob was planning on serving fried potatoes and onions to go with his cauliflower soup and warmed rolls for lunch that day.

That was when Jacob smiled at me for the first time. I said, "I'll see you tomorrow, Jacob! I know you just can't wait, can you? You're probably thinking, 'How did I end up with her in my kitchen?'"

He simply nodded, smiled, and gave me some chocolate chip cookies to take home. "For the kids," he said. Jacob had been listening, even though he wasn't saying much. He cared about my family. Washing up in the sink, I got a little teary at how blessed I was to be God-ordained to cook and clean. I felt happy to be the hands and feet of Jesus, and I was filled with amazement that God could be found so fully among fuzzy tomatoes and a silent but sensitive teacher.

Knowing that I was in the exact place God wanted me was a thrill like no other; but, as is typical with God, heaping helpings of pain were mixed in as well. I hadn't moved to Lexington alone. And as the months passed, and the leaves turned from green to red to brown, I watched the heart of my daughter Ty turn from adventure to anger. Far from her former friends, her extended family, and her normal way of life, Ty couldn't understand why we'd dragged her into something that seemed so foreign and fruitless.

She felt like her parents had abandoned their common sense, and God had abandoned her. And what was more, I couldn't blame her. Living missionly sounds great when you're forty, but quite frankly, when you're a teenager and you feel co-opted into the life, it's freaky. Nothing less, nothing more.

8

LOSING FAITH, LOSING LIMBS

I've learned a lot about what it means to live a missional life from my friend Sherry. *Missional* has become quite the buzzword, and there are as many definitions as there are ways to make bread. Here's mine: I look at my whole life as a mission from God. My life isn't divided between church and the real world, so everything I do ought to further the kingdom of God here on earth. It's a bit like thinking about yourself as a missionary/relief worker in your own hometown.

When I first understood that my life was a way to help fulfill God's mission to his creation, I was ready to pull out my hair. If everything I do matters, I have to worry about everything! There is no time off, morally or spiritually speaking. Shoot—I shouldn't waste time watching this mindless television program! Wait—should I even own a television? Egad—I just wasted time thinking about how I was wasting time!

Fortunately, real life is often colored in shades of gray, and God understands that the contours of our hearts often change at different rates. Some issues matter less than others, and most convictions come in stages. For instance, it took me a couple of years to conclude that where I buy my clothing matters. Eventually I stopped buying new clothing if I couldn't determine its origin. Since I can't afford most fair trade clothing, I shop at Goodwill and Sal's Boutique (as we call the Salvation Army Thrift Store at our house). These decisions happened gradually. I would never say you must do as I do, but neither would I compromise what I now understand to be a decision that influences the kingdom.

I know people who own only a few pieces of clothing. I know others who accelerate oh-so-slowly and run yellow lights so as not to be guilty of hogging the world's oil. My friends hang all of their laundry outside so as not to use as much coal. Right now I'm not there with them. But I understand what they're doing, and why, and I'm open to God's leading. I'm willing to change and be changed.

Our daily habits affect others, whether we realize it or not. Do we make choices that correspond with Jesus' admonition to love God and our neighbors as ourselves?

We try. We fail. We try again.

One member of our community describes it like this: "We're just trying to follow Jesus. We're giving it our best shot."

✿❧✿

Living with an awareness of others — neighbors, both local and global — can take its toll. I saw this firsthand at a Sunday fellowship gathering during our first year in Lexington.

Sherry asked for prayer. "My faith has hit bottom," she said, "and I need you guys to carry me through. I don't understand God anymore, or why any of this really matters."

I felt like I'd been punched in the stomach. Sherry was one of the most faithful Christians I'd ever known. She worked with refugees and was always around to lend a hand, whether you were putting in a garden or needed to be picked up at the airport. Building the kingdom was her first and seemingly only concern. I couldn't imagine what she was feeling. Even when I didn't understand or even like God (yes, I admitted that), red fear kept me hanging on to the basics of my faith — that I believed in Jesus and was pounding in my stake on his territory.

The next day we were enjoying the Labor Day party at our house. We're the party house — we can't help it. We love parties, and Will plays the host extraordinaire. Sherry and I sat down on the couch, and I asked her what happened to shake up her faith.

"I just don't know if I can believe all this anymore, Lisa. We try so hard to make a difference, and all this pain and horror goes on and God could make it all go away and he doesn't. It's monstrous."

Again: "What happened, Sherry?"

"I was taking Priscilla to the doctor." Priscilla is a Liberian refugee, a woman who saw loved ones massacred before her eyes, lived in the squalor of a refugee camp for years, and finally made it to America.

"She had this terrible lesion on her leg when I went over to see her. It hadn't healed for weeks, and I knew it was infected. I took her to the emergency room."

Liberia's official language is English, but Priscilla's grasp of American English wasn't strong. When civil war tore apart Priscilla's country, countless people were left with missing limbs (even babies weren't spared from the dreadful machetes of the rebels). Sherry told me that when the ER physician pointed to Priscilla's leg and explained they would have to clean the infection out of the wound, poor Priscilla thought the doctor was talking about amputation.

She went berserk. Wailing and screaming, thrown back to the days of horror she had survived, she thrashed and cried out. Imagine surviving such atrocities and reaching a place of safety only to be told you're going to be an amputee. I can only liken it to almost having a miscarriage —only to deliver a stillborn months later.

Sherry finally calmed her down and was able to communicate what the doctor had actually said. Another worker from the refugee ministry came to relieve Sherry, and she walked out of the hospital.

"Lisa, I walked to the parking lot. Nobody else was around. I looked up at the sky, at the stars, and I literally felt my faith drop out of me. Like coming over a hill too fast in a car, it just dropped into my stomach and was gone."

I listened while Sherry ranted at a God who would let Priscilla go through something like that. I didn't say that it wasn't God's fault. I let her speak about her disappointment, her disillusionment, and her anger—even anger at herself for serving for so many years for what now seemed like nothing.

It's easy to see our service as a raindrop in the ocean. What can one person do to help all those who suffer—the cancer patient, the battered woman, the grandmother with a drug-addicted daughter? Why does God allow all those poor children in Swaziland to be raped by their elders and infected with AIDS? How, in God's name, can he stand it?

If he's not going to do anything about it, why should we?

If you think you're about to read the answers to those questions, don't get your hopes up. The problem of evil and the sovereignty of God can't be tied into a tidy, satisfying bow. I believe God is good and God is sovereign. I know God is not the author of evil, but this world contains more evil than any of us have the capacity or the courage to imagine.

If you find a way to navigate this, please email me at *lisa@lisasamson. com*. (Unless your answer is, "Who are we to question God?"—to which I'd reply, "Human.")

Most mornings, I know that God loves me and that God loves those who suffer. Most days, because I love God I also want to love the people he loves. Most nights, I wonder why God chooses to love people through other people. Why he limits himself in this way is beyond me; I'm pretty sure I would never ask a fry cook to build my house or a pimp to babysit my kids.

෯෧ඓ෯෨

Early one Sunday morning, Phil, a mentally ill homeless man who was often angry, came by Sherry's house to demand a cup of coffee. Sherry saw Jesus in Phil—even if she wasn't sure she could see Jesus in herself anymore—and she handed him a mug of hot joe.

Every act of kindness, no matter how small, begins in the heart of God. Every act of kindness we offer another person becomes, somehow, a gift given back to God. Our faith rises like steam from a mug of hot coffee. It spins into the world, fading into nothing before our eyes.

But this is the mystery of faith: it rises again.

It rises when we serve a cup of kindness to those we like the least. It rises when, by grace alone, we feed and clothe and hold the child of God in front of us.

Thank God, like Sherry's faith eventually did, it rises again.

9

~~~~~~~~

MOVEABLE FEAST AND DYING MEN

God likes food. I don't know if he eats any himself. Jesus sure did. And apparently, he made some a time or two, lots of it, to share with the people who came to hear him. I imagine the bread he made and the fish he divided was about the best you could find. Maybe the provider of the five loaves and two fish took one bite and said, "This is better than it's ever tasted before."

When we moved into The Third Street House we figured we'd like to have Jesus at the table with us for meals. We correctly surmised he wasn't going to show up in a vision, so we figured he'd show up in human form, in that Matthew 25 way, needing food to eat or a beverage to drink. Maybe even more than that. So we set a sixth place, feeling a little silly, I might add, and waited with expectation. When Jesus showed up in Lexington, he was freshly "outed," kicked out of his home, and unable to go back to school for his junior year of college.

Jared joined us, rejected and full of pain and confusion. I don't know who I expected Jesus to be, but it wasn't a young gay man with gender confusion issues. Thankfully, we already knew Jared and knew what a loving person he was.

In our city there's a nonprofit organization called Moveable Feast Lexington that delivers dinner each weekday to AIDS patients and other housebound persons. We'd been in town about three months when I decided to volunteer there with Jared. Obviously God wanted me to get to know a little bit more about the gay community, so why not do something "outreachy"? Besides that, Jared might benefit from reaching out too. So we hopped in the car on Friday around suppertime and headed over to the ministry.

In the hot kitchen of the Episcopal church near the campus of the University of Kentucky, the head cook and his helpers spooned out portions into segmented Styrofoam containers. (I seriously considered stealing a piece of the roasted chicken but figured that would be a bad way to begin helping.) We placed the dinners in insulated duffel bags, zipped up the tops, and headed out to deliver the meals.

One client called himself Jacqueline. He wore a generous curly wig, flashy eye shadow, and a floral housedress. Jacqueline hadn't yet received his "gender reassignment" surgery, but the hormones had kicked in. I didn't understand Jacqueline, but that didn't change the fact that he needed a hot meal.

When someone is too far outside the realm of my previous experience, I try to remember that God isn't fazed one bit when he looks at us — and never mind our outsides! God loves all of us, from our curly wigs down to the deepest, darkest corners of our hearts.

Omnipresence means God is in Jacqueline's living room, just like he's in my car as I drive Jacqueline's meal over. And *divine love* means that God loves each of us, all the time, and there's nothing we can do or be to change that. When we start picking and choosing who deserves our help, the more we get to know people, the less deserving they'll be and — God, help us — the more prideful we'll become. "My sins aren't as bad," or "I'm not prone to such unwise decisions." Which is why we should, as Jesus said, work on the piece of firewood in our own eye before trying to get the toothpick out of someone else's.

We're all dying, and we all need help. Jacqueline happens to be dying of AIDS; I don't yet know what's killing me. I do know I need to show up at his house as the hands and feet of Jesus, and I know that someday it will be my turn to need that love.

Jesus came to save the sick, not the healthy. And the good news, believe it or not, is that *all of us are sick.*

Now, to be honest, I took Jared with me so that he might see firsthand what could happen to him if he failed to be careful sexually. It was my object lesson for the importance of chastity. How self-righteous I was! Where would somebody take me to learn what they think I need? Helping people with their anger-management issues? Or down to an arts center in order to encourage people not to squander their gifts? I can think of a lot more, but they're between God and me.

Several years later, Jared is doing well. He's on his own two feet and trying, each day, to hear the voice of God. Sometimes I think the Holy Spirit should tell him the same things I would. But God is more patient with Jared than I am. And God is more patient with me than I deserve.

Now excuse me while I go looking for a hefty pair of tongs to pull out that firewood.

10

FAILURE BY DISAPPOINTMENT

After living in Lexington for six months, I began to look forward to seeing Jacob in the kitchen.

The ice broke when Jacob caught me dancing to Pink while cooking at the range.

"Caught you!" he said, laughing.

"I'm sorry you had to witness that," I replied with a smirk. As Ty will tell you, I'm not much of a dancer. The sad thing is, I think I've got some moves, but everybody around me thinks my efforts are hilarious.

"She my girl!" Jacob said. "That Pink is my girl!"

Amid the soapsuds and the soup preparation, we began to talk more about our lives, what the kids were getting into, my writing. He liked to set muffins or cupcakes aside for the kids.

When the CAC asked me to help in the warehouse instead of the shelter—they wanted to sell donated books online—it kept me out of the shelter's kitchen for about a month. I thought of Jacob often, but despite many nudges to visit him, I never did.

When I finally made it back to the kitchen, Jacob wasn't there. A man I'd never seen was standing in Jacob's place, doing Jacob's chores. I hurried out front and asked Aaron, the desk attendant, "Where's Jacob?"

He shook his head. "He's gone. Went back on cocaine."

I'd been ready to do whatever it took to serve the poor. I was helping wherever I was asked, I was praying, and I was building relationships

—wasn't that exactly what I was supposed to do? And wasn't obedience supposed to produce good fruit?

My willing heart fell into the pit of my stomach, and I walked out of the building. To this day, I haven't stepped foot in the CAC. I can't. Something inside of me has taken over and said, "Just do the clean work. Somebody has to lick envelopes and answer phones. That's part of handing out justice too."

I wasn't prepared for failure. Geoff and Sherry, and so many others in our community and other communities, told me my heart would be broken. I was told I'd feel like a failure, just schlepping along, trying to help but finding that 90 percent of my efforts seemed useless.

But I didn't believe it. I was programmed to believe there was always a formula for success. Worse, I believed success was a barometer of whether or not God was blessing me. We tell ourselves the big stories, the successes, and act like that's the norm.

The opposite is true. The kingdom of heaven is like a mustard seed, a hidden treasure, a lost coin — *small* things. All we can do is pray that these small things bloom one day. In the meantime, our knees ache, and we wonder what God is playing at.

So I began driving Naila around town instead. Naila came from Russia as a refugee with her husband, her little boy, and a sister. When I would pick her up at her apartment to run her to medical appointments, an old Russian grandmother would sometimes come out into the yard. She was dressed pretty much like you'd imagine — full skirt, long-sleeved blouse, and a head scarf. We'd just smile at one another; I don't speak Russian, and Grandmother didn't speak English.

I hear a lot of talk about immigrants learning to speak English. "If you want to live in America, learn to speak the language, darn it!" I used to say that too, until I met some of those immigrants who are strangers in this land. The Bible has much to say about the stranger. Listen to the way Job describes righteous living:

> Whoever heard me spoke well of me,
> > and those who saw me commended me,

because I rescued the poor who cried for help,
    and the fatherless who had none to assist him.
The man who was dying blessed me;
    I made the widow's heart sing.
I put on righteousness as my clothing;
    justice was my robe and my turban.
I was eyes to the blind
    and feet to the lame.
I was a father to the needy;
    I took up the case of the stranger.
I broke the fangs of the wicked
    and snatched the victims from their teeth.

Job 29:11–17

Has God changed all that much?

Jesus knew what it was like to live as a stranger and to invite strangers into his company. What if we who claim to follow Jesus did the same? Perhaps the stranger on your block escaped his country with his life even as he lost a limb; perhaps she watched as her children were kidnapped and forced to become savage soldiers. Perhaps that couple is supporting an entire family back home, so they each work two full-time jobs at less than minimum wage.

This is not about political beliefs. As followers of the Son of God — the Son who left the glories of heaven to become human — we might try, at the very least, to imagine ourselves in the worn shoes of the strangers in our country. Is there room in our hearts to love the stranger as God does?

In Matthew 25, Jesus calls his followers to care for strangers, telling us that when we welcome the stranger, we welcome *him*. As the writer of the letter to the Hebrews says in chapter 13 verse 2, "Do not forget to entertain strangers, for by so doing some people have entertained angels without knowing it." I don't know about you, but that sounds exciting! Imagine someday meeting an angel in heaven who says, "We were stranded out on I–40. We knew a bunch of Christians would be on their way to church that morning, but *you* were the one who stopped. Thank you." Another angel nods. "I was with him, strapped in the car seat. You filled my sippy cup with some of the orange juice you were going to be serving during the coffee hour after Sunday school."

Or, "You saw us encamped after we picked strawberries, and you came over and asked how we were doing. You gave me dignity just by acknowledging my presence as a fellow human."

We never know, so let's love lavishly.

Naila and I zipped around town twice a week for about a year. She needed a lot of dental work and was on government assistance for her care (and as someone without dental insurance, I had some pretty nasty, selfish thoughts — but you learn to live with those and shove them aside), and then became pregnant with her second son. Off to the ob-gyn every month. We never could really say much due to my nonexistent knowledge of the Russian language. Our conversation went like this each time:

"Hi, Naila! How are you?"

"Fine. How are you?"

"Great." I nodded. A lot. And tried to put big, friendly sparkles on the surface of my dark blue eyes. I'd sweep my hand across the windshield. "Beautiful weather," I'd say.

"Yes." She'd nod and smile, and there were big, friendly sparkles on her eyes.

Four times out of ten, I'd stop for gas and a Coke. "Something to drink?" I'd flip up a cupped hand in the international sign for drinking.

She always refused.

"Your son? Is he good?"

"Oh. Yes. Yes."

We'd head into the medical offices, where I'd make sure the staff knew who she was, what she'd come for, and what was going on. Most people were friendly and courteous. Some bit their tongues, their mouths pinched, the muscles petrifying beneath their cheeks, their verbiage clipped. Some shook their heads. Maybe they didn't have dental insurance either.

Eventually she gave birth to a beautiful boy, and soon we were driving to the pediatrician's office for checkups. It was good for me to see Naila with her baby, his skin fresh and soft, his clothes always bright and clean. That Christmas, I dropped Naila off after another doctor's visit.

"Wait. I have gift for you."

I watched her slender frame retreat into the apartment townhouse. She favored a pink, cable-knit sweater, her long, dark hair falling in a ponytail against the blushing garment. When she returned with something in her hands, her brown eyes shot off extra sparkles. "For you. We make."

She settled a round loaf of homemade bread into my hands. I cried, "Thank you, Naila!" gushing my appreciation for a good thirty seconds. My heart was full. She'd made that bread with her hands and her time. It was the best loaf of bread I've ever tasted.

Sometimes life slips through a person's clinging fingers, and the net of your love cannot catch him; sometimes a person you love in Jesus' name grabs on to life and refuses to let go.

The line between fresh bread and cocaine addiction is thin. Only God knows who will live and who will die. I don't like this, but I know it is true. I've learned to leave those matters in his hands.

If I hadn't, I'd have never survived what Swaziland would reveal.

11

⟨⟨⟨ ⟩⟩⟩

JOSE CARLOS, A SODA,
AND A POSSIBLE THEOPHANY

If you expect Jesus to show up by setting an extra place at the table, you can bet he'll show up in other places as well.

One night after our community's Sunday night gathering, Gwynnie and I decided to walk home. It was a gorgeous evening in early autumn. About a block from our house, a man approached us and asked for seventy cents so he could buy a can of soda. We don't give money to strangers—normally I don't carry cash, so it's easy to say this.

Since we weren't far from home, I said, "We live right down the street. How 'bout we just give you a cup of soda?"

The man agreed, and I whispered to Gwynnie, "Go tell Daddy to have a cup of soda ready for this guy." She ran off down the sidewalk.

He stood about five foot five, spoke with a Hispanic accent, and had glistening black eyes with too much moisture. He shoved his hands into the pockets of his faded jeans and walked by my side. The sneakers on his feet had obviously gone miles and back many times over, so half a block would mean nothing.

Will met us with a bottle of soda and three cups, and we sat down on the front porch.

"So what's your name?" Will asked, easing himself into our rocking chair.

"Why do you want to know?" Translation: "I'm an illegal alien."

"Oh, just asking."

He peered at both of us, his suspicion as loud as the bass beat of a passing car. "Jose."

We introduced ourselves as he sipped.

Our cat Coltrane oozed by delicately. The feline is a fat, orange, striped mass of animal. Jose eyed him. "I do not eat cats."

"Well, that's a good place to start," said Will.

"I do not eat humans either."

I was relieved. I realized Jose wasn't running on a full tank, but this was the most bizarre conversation I'd ever heard. Will acted as though he'd talked with three people just last week who didn't eat cats. Or humans for that matter.

Jose's glassy eyes looked toward the street. "I was born in a barn with only a blanket."

Poor guy, I thought. Must have experienced poverty firsthand. Did his mom do the best she could? Where was his father in all of this? How did he get to Lexington, Kentucky?

"Where are you from?" I asked.

"Why do you ask these questions?"

Yikes. Obviously, I was navigating new waters. I'd never thought of that question as remotely controversial. "I'm just interested in where you're from and all. Just making conversation, I guess." Just out of my element, for sure.

"Oh." He told us about his daughter and pulled out a little picture. "If you opened my head and looked inside, there would be nothing there. My brain is in pieces all over the world."

I realized then he was either totally off his rocker or strung out. Or a poet. (Will figured the moment he saw him that Jose was tripping. Like I said, I'm slow about this stuff.)

"Interesting." Will continued rocking.

"I was tortured for the sake of the world." Jose became very grave.

We made more very odd small talk about the nice autumn we were having, how a cold soda on a warm day feels just right, why at least three people a day go the wrong way down our one-way street.

Gwynnie appeared every now and again, making sure we were OK, I suppose, then disappearing back into the house.

"By the way," Jose said. "My middle name is Carlos." He said this with a nod of satisfaction, a knowing expression, and a nod. He presented it like a gift, holding the name before us as if we should give it a hug and a kiss.

After he took off, carrying the remainder of the two-liter bottle, I pulled Will aside. "Oh, my gosh. Can you believe that? *JC*? Tortured for the sake of the world? The blanket and stuff?"

"And he doesn't eat cats or humans."

Will doesn't look for the mystical in everything like I do.

"You gotta admit," I pressed, "it's really weird. Do you think that was a theophany?"

"No, I don't. But if theophanies still happened, I have a feeling they would look just like that."

To this day I wonder if Jesus really did show up that night, or, at the very least, if we were entertaining an angel. And in that wondering I am blessed. Who really gets to wonder if they gave Christ the remainder of a two-liter bottle of Pepsi?

12

⌇⌇⌇⌇⌇

TRULY PRO-LIFE

As a writer and a person with a growing passion to communicate with other Christians about justice and compassion, I've volunteered at a lot of places in order to get a feel for what life is like for as many struggling people as I can.

The autumn before we left for Swaziland, I began working at a home for single teen mothers here in Lexington. It takes them in, cares for them during their pregnancies, and then, if they choose to mother their child themselves, provides a space for them to keep their child and attend high school right on campus.

All this, and the workers never raise their voices to the girls, never shame them, never try to coerce their cooperation by anger or guilt. The staff keeps a chart on which each girl gets a check mark for finishing her chores and living up to her responsibilities. If she doesn't, no trip to the mall or the movies. Consistency is the key. (A lot of us could learn from them about how to deal with teenagers!)

I found out about this opportunity to volunteer at the home for teen moms on *www.volunteermatch.org*. If you're looking for a way to plug into your community, head on over there, type in your zip code, and you'll unearth more possibilities than you'll know what to do with. And many of them will fit your personality. Hey, I'm an introvert. I write alone for the most part. Even my hobbies — reading, art, and needlework — are solitary. I'm much more comfortable in a supporting role — cooking, answering phones, licking envelopes. Helping justice roll down takes many hands, many types of people.

This women's home needed someone to answer their phones. But let me warn you — even when you do simple things, such as answering phones, you're still becoming part of other people's lives, and life is never simple.

I'll never forget Katy, a sixteen-year-old from eastern Kentucky. When I saw her, her strawberry hair fell well past her shoulders in a glorious, shiny swatch that swung against her scapulae. Her features were even, and her expression was bland, almost blank. I'd never seen such a closed affect on someone. It was as if stimuli flowed by her like water over river rock.

The director told me her story when I commented on her beautiful hair. "When she came here, her hair was filled with lice. She wasn't at all taken care of at home. And her baby, well — Katy had no idea how to take care of a newborn. Her parents were no help. When she came here, the baby was eight months old and weighed only eight pounds. Katy was feeding her pudding and orange juice."

I felt my heart drop. I've always been pro-life. I believe human life begins at conception and should end with natural death. But Katy and her baby fell beyond the traditional scope of pro-life concerns once the baby was born alive and sent home from the hospital.

Katy scarcely seemed aware of her baby. What made Katy that way? What actions or words of others slowly encircled her, fencepost by fencepost, then shut the gate? I almost don't want to know. It's just one more thing I'd have to ask God about, and I don't want to screw up the good place God and I are in right now.

Looking at that sweet baby with red hair like her mama's triggered something in me. I realized that for years I had been pro-*birth* more than pro-*life*—I didn't want any pre-born babies to die, but I hardly thought about their life after birth. I always pooh-poohed criticism from people who said it was hypocritical to care only about the child's right to be born but not the right to live a life with enough food, a roof over her head, and adequate medical care. That was beside the point, I always replied. Since birth is foundational, that was my first concern.

I looked at Katy and her child and saw my myopia. If not for this women's home where I was working, that baby might have died. Is a grave holding a tiny casket really any different from a bag of fetal tissue in a clinic garbage can? And who am I to decide that it is?

13

◈◈◈

HOUSE OF HOSPITALITY AND CLUELESSNESS

Near the beginning of this book, I invited you into our "house of hospitality." I must admit, we use the term loosely. Dorothy Day, the founder of the Catholic Worker Movement, might cross her arms and say, *"That's a house of hospitality? I don't see addicts or the down-and-out coming in at all hours of the day."* True, but she wasn't helping her three kids get their homework done at night.

When I talk about our hospitality, think more of the Southern woman who loves to have folks over for iced tea or a delicious meal—except we're not choosy about who gets in. We figure Jesus was serious when he talked about the king throwing a banquet and inviting people off the streets (Luke 14:16–24). Decent folk had all sorts of excuses for why they couldn't come—and honestly, the excuses sound pretty good. I've used them myself: business affairs, parental care. Jesus didn't tell a story with weak excuses. He accused people of letting good things get in the way of something better—joining the King at his banquet. There goes Jesus again.

Jesus knew that sometimes we need to set aside our common sense. Let's face it, those people he ended up inviting were probably not the safest of people.

Our house parties are peopled with folks from all walks of life— university department chairs, authors, missionaries, clergy, social workers, retail managers and workers, homeless people, and folks in halfway houses trying to figure things out. A group of homeless guys always finds out about our parties. One is loudmouthed and rude, and every time he shows up to eat, he leaves without ever saying thank you. Jesus would probably go sit with him, but I've got to work the charcoal grill, right? (I hide behind menial labor, in case you haven't noticed, but we all jump in where we can swim and move slowly to deeper waters.)

Jesus also told his followers to be "as shrewd as snakes and as innocent as doves" (Matthew 10:16). I'm not sure exactly what that looks like, but I can tell you what it *doesn't* look like: me! So many times, when people hear God's call to make the world a more just place (because that sort of thing is important to him), they let their hearts get ahead of their heads. "I'll just help anybody who asks and let God sort out the details."

There's nothing wrong with that at first. Let's face it, at the beginning we have more energy — more verve from which to serve anybody and everybody who comes our way. However, when you live in a house with a husband and daughter who have the gift of discernment, you end up feeling a little goofy.

In other words, I've been taken for a ride by several people since opening our house of hospitality. I couldn't help it. They seemed so sad, so down-and-out. One man, let's call him Carl, was even on dialysis. I recognized the fistula in his arm and knew that part of the story was the truth. (My mom died of a kidney disease.) The poor guy needed groceries and some work. Of course I could help. I'd just buy the groceries, not hand out money.

The morning after I met him, I hopped in my station wagon and headed over to pick him up. We talked on the journey. He was new to Lexington, had moved around a lot — nothing specific about his past other than he had grown up in Pikeville, where his mother was still living. He thanked me for the groceries and asked if I had a little yard work for him to do — he'd won awards up in Michigan for his yard work, he said.

He mowed the yard the next day.

Soon old Carl and I had a regular schedule going. He'd come up with a convincing story about rent or medical supplies, and off we'd drive to the ATM for a twenty.

Hundreds of dollars and many lies later, Carl was in our living room pleading for help. His mother was sick, and he had to get to Pikeville. He needed gas money to go east, and a friend was willing to drive. I gave him fifty dollars.

After Carl left, Will finally sat me down and gently said, "He's lying, Lisa. If I can't convince you, let me just call the hospital or the assisted living home in Pikeville to check out his story." He did. Of course, there was no woman by the name Carl had given us.

I was crushed.

Still I soldiered on. His requests became smaller and smaller until one evening he said he needed ten dollars to buy a lock for his lawnmower.

"I'll buy you the lock, Carl." I wasn't going to give him a dime again.

He became agitated as we drove toward the Rite-Aid. He always called me Miss Lisa—and I hated it. Carl was in his fifties. I told him to call me Lisa, but he persisted. Finally I pulled over, put the car in park, and confronted him.

"What do you really want the money for, Carl?"

"I swear I'm telling the truth, Miss Lisa."

Something wasn't right about a fifty-year-old African-American man ingratiating himself to me. I wanted to weep. I couldn't keep up with his deception. The best thing I could do, although all my natural instincts toward love and compassion cried out against it, was to stop giving. I hated it.

"You're lying to me, Carl. I'm not moving until you tell me what you really want this money for."

"Miss Lisa, I met a lady at church today. A nice lady. I just wanted to take her to Kentucky Fried for a chicken dinner. I can make ten dollars go a long way, yes I can!"

"Carl, do you realize when you lie to me like that it's like you're slapping me in the face? I want to help you, but you can't lie to people, Carl."

He was contrite as we headed toward the ATM. I knew I was supposed to love him in tangible ways, but I didn't know how to anymore.

When I stopped in front of his apartment and handed him a ten dollar bill, he said, "No more lies, Miss Lisa. Straight talk from here on out."

"Good for you, Carl. Have a nice time."

I never saw Carl again. I think he moved away.

"He realized he'd probably used up his capital here in Lexington and skipped town," Will said. "He's probably lived like this for years, baby."

I still wonder where he is.

I'm a descendant of slaveholders in Virginia. I see the down-and-out members of the black community here in Lexington, and I drive around in my paid-off Volvo wagon from my other life, and something inside me says, "Their ancestors' blood, sweat, and tears helped make me what I am today."

A hundred chicken dinners from Kentucky Fried won't even that score.

Do thoughts like that make me a bleeding-heart liberal? If you say so. And I'm OK with that.

14

❧❧❧

BRING OUT YOUR DEAD

When God takes you to a new place, don't begin to expect to know what he's going to do with you. I pictured something akin to a mission on skid row, but God had something else in mind entirely. In Jeremiah 29, God tells exiled Israel to settle down in their new place—to marry, build houses, and plant gardens. The members of *communality* take that injunction seriously. Why God gathered us, from many areas of the country and overseas, to exile in Lexington is something we'll be trying to figure out and work on for years to come.

So we've married and built households, and in the past two years or so, planting gardens has become one of the chief missions of our community. There's nothing that shows the lavish abundance of God like good food—beautiful crimson tomatoes bursting with juice, cheerful pumpkins and squash, slender beans climbing up poles, deep-pink beets and golden potatoes nesting in the earth. We're of the crazy opinion that proper nutrition will do a world of good for those living in want, that good food will help children in school, that vitamin-rich produce will help parents assume their responsibilities.

I don't want you to assume that I have a lot to do with this. This is an area of our community in which Will has taken the role of family representative. But the more he is involved, the more chores I take on here at the home front. (Sometimes works of justice include taking on mundane responsibilities to allow your significant other to spread his wings. It isn't sexy, but it is necessary when you're running a household.)

❧❧❧

The London Ferrell Community Garden is a place where Sherry, Ryan and Jodie, Will, and other members of *communality* are bringing back life from death and honoring a man who was Jesus to so many people almost two hundred years ago.

I'll get us another cup of tea before I tell you the story.

In 1833, a cholera epidemic broke out in Lexington. The streets were deserted, except for the death carts. Bodies, some in wooden boxes, trunks, or wrapped in the bedclothes on which they had died, were piled at the entrances of the city graveyards awaiting burial, stacked like so many pieces of firewood. (Reading accounts of the time period, I'm chilled by the similarity to the AIDS epidemic.) Six weeks later, the disease had run its course, leaving five hundred people dead in its wake.

Our society has a hard time processing numbers. Our nation is nine trillion dollars in debt, yet we are completely unable to understand how much money that really is. Twelve million children have been orphaned by AIDS in sub-Saharan Africa. We fail to comprehend the implications of such mammoth figures. At least I do.

Five hundred people dead is a lot. It's two hundred and fifty sets of parents; it's children from hundreds of families. From one family of nineteen only two sons survived the scourge. Some people fled the city, while others stayed away from the public square. Life came to a standstill.

London Ferrell lived in Lexington during the epidemic. As pastor of the First Baptist Church of Colored Persons, he saw his fair share of death. We can assume he buried people on a regular basis, and from what I surmise about his behavior during the epidemic, he took Christian burial very seriously.

London Ferrell, a freed slave, was listed in records as a "waiter." But he'd been preaching in private homes and churches since he was a young man. He was called by many of the wealthy to perform funerals when one of their servants died. London Ferrell was well acquainted with death before the cholera epidemic struck on June 1, 1833.

His biography tells us that he was the only preacher left in the city and that he said prayers over all the dead—white and black alike. The same people who wouldn't allow Preacher Ferrell into their church were buried by him in the name of Christ. When all the white clergy fled the city, it was Reverend London Ferrell from the First Baptist Church of Colored People who laid the dead in the ground.

During the epidemic, Reverend Ferrell buried his own wife. How he continued on, still loving God and preaching and pastoring, I can only guess. His hope in God must have been compelling, and his strength must have flowed from the power of the Holy Spirit. Death gave Reverend Ferrell the opportunity to serve Jesus in Lexington when no one else would.

Almost every day, I drive by the corner of Third and Rose and the Old Episcopal Burying Ground, final resting place for many of the cholera victims. It's a peaceful place actually; normally the gates are locked, keeping out the passersby. Something about that corner is sacred. Maybe it's left over from London Ferrell's selfless act of serving those who lie beneath the mown grass of the graveyard, a reminder of what happens when one person simply follows the Lord and doesn't hold sin in his heart. Maybe it's left over from the forgiveness this man must have practiced to have been able to do what he did.

Sometimes I'll see Ryan tilling a garden patch or some of the neighbors in the area working on their plots, picking peppers, hoeing along the rows of squashes and cabbages. Black and white together for the common purpose of growing food—something we all need. Seeds of reconciliation are being sown in the London Ferrell Community Garden. One hundred and seventy years later, people till plots and plant seeds in the hope that what has become a racially divided neighborhood will grow together in the spirit of London Ferrell and his legacy of love and forgiveness. It's amazing what a little food can do. It's understandable why God told Israel to plant gardens and settle in.

Pastor Ferrell not only blazed the trail for our community gardeners; he blazed the trail for me as well. I could only speculate that Swaziland, with its staggering HIV/AIDS rate, with its burial rate, was much like the cholera epidemic of 1833. But London Ferrell inspires me, along with the tale of a missionary in Swaziland who did one funeral every couple of weeks when he landed in Africa twelve years ago. That number would be shocking to a Western clergyman. Imagine if every pastor in your town had a funeral to officiate every two weeks. To make matters worse, and there always seems to be a worse in an AIDS-ravaged country, this missionary now does twelve to fifteen funerals *a day*. Burying the dead has become his primary ministry. He's the London Ferrell of Swaziland, I suppose.

Even as food grew beside a place of the dead, tendrils sprouting from the deep, brown earth that also covers the grave, I knew Swaziland would hold the same kind of mystery for me, the same lessons. How does life come from death? And isn't that the gospel story, isn't that what we celebrate in the Eucharist—Christ's body and Christ's blood, offered up in death, food and drink for the hungry and thirsty soul? I could only pray the gospel story wouldn't fall short when death was literally staring me in the eyes.

THE COMMISSION

Ty

If you had met me five years ago, you would've met a different person. I measured and weighed in pretty much the same as I do now, but my dreams were different. I would have told you all about how I wanted to live in New York, become an architect, wear all the latest fashions — or even better, high-priced vintage clothing. It was a bad Sex and the City

impersonation, but I wanted it — and at fourteen, I believed I would do anything to make that life my own. I wanted glamour and romance and thought nothing could stand in the way of that dream.

I was already well on my way. As Mom mentioned, we lived in a large house in the suburbs, rode around in two nice cars, and enjoyed a sufficient expendable income. While we weren't as materialistic as many, we still lived in a bubble—a shiny bubble that kept us unaware of any trouble in the world, save for the things that happened to us or our friends. We ate well, we redecorated our home when we wanted to, we traveled. I would be lying if I said a part of me doesn't miss that life these days.

But that lifestyle comes with a price.

Every morning, my father would wake up at 3:45 so he could get ready in time to catch the train into D.C. His commute totaled almost four hours a day, and by the time he came through the door, exhaustion weighed him down. So while we had many nice things, we missed out on time with him. I'm close to my father. I needed him more than I needed the mall or a new CD.

When my parents first began going through these changes, I wondered what was going to happen and where all this would land me, my brother, and my sister. There were times I resented my mom and dad—and God—for the upheaval. But now I have a new life, new goals. All this comes at a cost, however. I guess our choices, for good or bad, always do.

It wasn't until our third year in Lexington, a lot of resentment filling my heart, that I truly began to realize why God had exiled us to a place that felt so foreign at first.

Claudia, my godmother and one of my mom's best friends, was visiting us, a woman God brought into my life to love me and encourage me in ways no one else can. She is the least condemning, critical person I know. Miss Claudia said that she wanted to bless us and do a foot washing. I mentioned it earlier, but let me set the scene.

After dinner, we all assembled in the living room, and she brought a bowl of warm, soapy water. I remember her washing

Gwynnie's and Jake's feet and telling them beautiful, poetic things in a way that only she can. And then Miss Claudia moved on to me.

She took my feet in her beautiful hands and started speaking to me in a soft voice. When she began talking, I could immediately feel the Holy Spirit enter the room. I felt like everything that had been weighing me down was being lifted off my body, and I was bawling within seconds. If you know me at all, you know that I never cry. I could count on one hand the number of times I cried. But on this warm spring evening, I cried more than I've ever cried before. It was like God was opening up my eyes to the hurt in the world, yet doing it in such a loving way. She told me I would work with the people no one wants to work with. The dirty, the forgotten. People nobody even thinks to care for.

The rest of that night is still a blur to me. After Miss Claudia was done blessing us, I went upstairs and cried for another two hours before writing down in my journal everything that occurred that night. It was then I realized God's path for me. Just living downtown and giving people food occasionally wasn't good enough for me. I needed to be with the poorest of the poor.

First stop: Africa.

Journey to Africa

WHAT WOULD I LEAVE BEHIND?

Ty

Two weeks to go, and I was scared. I had all that I needed for the trip — lots of T-shirts and long skirts. We had gotten all the shots we needed, and our passports were good to go. But this was such a huge and complicated journey. All the things that could go wrong raced through my mind. What if our plane went down? What if Mom and I got separated somehow? What if we came down with an illness or were injured and ended up in a backwoods hospital? What would Gwynnie, Jake, and Dad do if we died?

My pessimistic thoughts couldn't stall our trip, although at times I wished they would. Maybe I could find an excuse to stay home. My own bed seemed especially cozy, and nobody cooks like my dad. Besides, I needed to get that English paper done, right?

Finally, on a cold January morning, Mom and I woke up, packed our bags in the car, and left for Louisville Airport. That's when things started to go wrong.

Our flight to Chicago was cancelled, but the flight attendant thought we could still reach Washington Dulles Airport in time to board our flight to Johannesburg, South Africa. So we hung around the airport, drinking coffee and taking pictures. We caught a later flight to Chicago and hung around some more, as our connecting flight kept getting delayed further and further out. When they called our flight, our backs were sore, and we were more than ready to board.

At last we landed in Washington, D.C., with almost no time to spare. I looked at Mom, wondering how we were going to make it. She said, "Get ready to run!"

However, irony was really working in high gear. Delayed on the tarmac and unable to deplane, we could see our plane to Johannesburg parked two gates down. I pictured all the people we'd invited to come with us, getting on board that flight and, with high levels of excitement, having a great time chatting about what they'd see. And here we were, so close and yet so helpless.

The flight attendant allowed my mom and me, along with Kevin and Christy, a married couple who were also going with Children's HopeChest, to sit in empty seats in first class so that when the doors opened we could be the first to exit. The instant those doors opened, we took off running. It felt like a bad romantic comedy with all of us flying through the airport, but we were determined to make our flight. I could picture a stopwatch in my head, clicking down the minutes. I thought my mom was going to keel over. Christy was hanging on to her pillow, while Kevin's hair, a mass of long brown curls, looked like it was going to fly off his head.

The four of us finally skidded into the gate, only to find the King of Smarm working at the South African Airlines desk and taking a considerable amount of pleasure in telling us the flight had left just five minutes earlier. Five. Minutes.

Couldn't they have held the plane just a couple of minutes longer? As the King assured us, no, in fact, they couldn't, I wanted to punch the guy. We'd planned, prayed, plotted, and dreamed for months. Mom reminded me what it was like to be a refugee, how people all over the world are inconvenienced like this on a daily basis, but at the time I wasn't ready to learn any kind of lesson.

Later that evening, we flew to England and spent much of the next day in Heathrow Airport. We drank lots of coffee, window-shopped in the terminal stores, read magazines, embroidered, and chatted with Kevin and Christy, already creating a bond in our travel distresses. Finally, we heard the call and boarded our plane to Johannesburg.

This flight felt like every minute took an hour. Sitting behind a screaming child for eleven hours is not fun. Mom said she'd never had homicidal thoughts toward a toddler before that — she does not do well without sleep.

We arrived in South Africa, relieved but exhausted, only to find that our luggage was missing.

Honestly, by that time our anger dissolved into laughter. What next?

When Jumbo Gerber, who, along with his wife, Kriek, works for Children's HopeChest and who is the one who arranged our trip on the ground in Swaziland, appeared to collect us, he looked better than Jude Law holding a triple fudge sundae. Even with Jumbo's South African reserve, we felt like we'd been plunged back into someplace warm and normal.

We were finally heading to Swaziland! After connecting with the rest of our group in Jo'burg, we piled into vans and rumbled off. The three-hour drive, after everything we had been through, seemed like nothing. Before we knew it, we were in Manzini, Swaziland, climbing out of the vans, collecting our things, and chatting our way into our lodging. A bed never looked so good.

I was thankful to be in Africa. Around three in the afternoon, I took a nap and didn't wake up until the next morning.

I'd need the rest. If I thought missed planes and disappointment were bad, what I was about to see would reduce the significance of our journey there to the level of having to order Pepsi instead of Coke. I was in for the experience of my life.

15

❧❧❧❧

IT'S NEVER EASY, IS IT?

There are countless ways to die in Swaziland, but most likely it's HIV/AIDS that will get someone. The HIV infection rate in this small kingdom — the last true kingdom in Africa — is nearly four out of ten. Swaziland is cursed with the highest rate of AIDS infection in the world.

What do you think such statistics *look* like?

As I read and dreamed and prayed about Swaziland, I pictured skeletal waifs lining the sides of the road, Ping-Pong ball eyes protruding above sharp cheekbones. I imagined desperate squalor and filth, and tears and sadness streaking every face.

Instead, much to my surprise, I saw men and women in brightly colored garb traveling the roads with cows, cows, cows. Cows are everywhere, roaming free, and somehow — it seemed like magic to me — everyone knows which cow belongs to whom. Cows are currency. Thirteen cows for a bride. Ask Dennis, our American guide, who was preparing to marry a Swazi lady.

Outside the homes — mostly two- or three-room stick, stone, and mud houses with tin roofs — clotheslines wave clean garments in the sunshine. Another surprise for me — how clean and bright the clothing of the people. Skirts flutter in the breeze in greens and reds; purple headscarves and blue or yellow shirts soak up the sun. It's amazing how we can be so misinformed about people living in poverty — assuming that they're dirty slackers with no pride whatsoever, that lack of resources automatically demands clothing layered with sweat and dirt, hands outlined with grime.

The children walked along the roads shimmering with heat, smiling when Dennis would honk and wave to them. The longer he stays in this land, the more famous and expected his blaring horn, earnest waves, and shouts of "Yebo!" become. It's a greeting, much like "Hey, man!" here in the States. "Yebo" is cool. No matter where we humans are, cool is cool. Even in a country where death is ever-present, we find ways to keep living—and make life a little brighter in the process.

But these colorful scenes aren't romantic, or even very realistic. Do these kids know their life expectancy is thirty-two? Or that if they are orphaned, they probably won't live past their fifteenth birthday?

I hope not.

It's difficult to live knowing death might overtake you at any moment. Just as I wonder if my heart will speed up into that crazy rhythm and leave me lifeless before I can reach the hospital, do these kids wonder if HIV is hiding somewhere inside their bodies just waiting to blossom?

I hope not.

As they walk the valley roads between the green, rolling mountains —some pushing wheelbarrows with water jugs inside, others in school uniforms—I can only hope they're simply thinking about the next few hours. Who can blame them if that's all they can do?

They've seen more than I have, with my pipe dreams of making a difference. They've seen their mother or father, aunt or uncle, brother or sister or neighbor hidden away in the back room of their house, or a house nearby. They know that death was said to come in the form of some disease —sugar diabetes, cancer, tuberculosis, pneumonia. But most likely they know the truth—that AIDS is stealing away their family. I pray that the children think they'll be the ones who will escape the possibility of death by AIDS.

Just as I pray I will escape death from WPW.

But what overlap is there between their lives and mine? My chance of living is high, and their chance of dying is even higher. What can we possibly bring? What will we learn? Where, in this bright, dying place, is hope? Where can it be found when sickness is denied, death a place of shame, and the grave a place from which no life is allowed to blossom?

16

❦❧❦❧

ISAIAH 58, *AGAIN?*

Our first morning in Swaziland, we ate a good breakfast — salami, smoked salmon, a hard-cooked egg, watermelon, an apricot, a fried egg, and a piece of toast with apricot jam. Coffee. Small bits of each item, but even on our first day in-country we understood that it was more than we deserved or needed.

We were divided into two distinct groups. One group was there to help at carepoints, the places where children come to eat, learn, and be discipled. At each carepoint, older women — *gogos*, the Swazi word for "grandmother" — cook two meals a day for the kids.

The second group, our group, consisted of Tom Davis, the president of CHC; several friends, including author (and Ty's godmother), Claudia Mair Burney; Andrea Christian, a publishing professional; and our guide, missionary Dennis Brock. Carepoints, orphanages, hospitals, villages, schools — we were there to be exposed, to be broken in two, to remember and record.

Tom opened his Bible and began to read from Isaiah 58.

Sometimes I get the feeling God likes beating me over the head. Probably because I need it.

Ty and I locked eyes. God keeps sending me this message because I keep doing a half-baked job of following. "Expend your life on behalf of the poor"? *Expend* means being worn-out, dried-up, caved-in, broken-down, melted, sapped, burned, and tattered, my inner self whirling away like ash in a scorching breeze. I told Claudia about the significance of the reading, saying, "I'm toast."

"You are," she replied, hiking her bag higher up on her shoulder in the already increasing heat of the morning.

Great.

I thought I'd been catching on in Lexington, but here were those verses again. The big verse that got me to leave my home and my old life. What was God asking of me that I hadn't given already?

JUMPING AND DANCING

Ty

I could barely eat the dinner placed before me the next night. I have to admit, I wasn't feeling worthy, not after meeting the kids we visited that day. The table was clothed in white linen; the menu was filled with items such as fillets, quail, and Wiener schnitzel. Cold beverages were offered. It was one of the nicest places in Swaziland. Choking back feelings of distress, I picked up my soup spoon and tried to forget long enough to eat.

Earlier, our first morning in Swaziland, we all ate breakfast together. It was an eclectic group of people that morning. We had pastors, CEOs, writers, editors, moms, and children. The ages ranged from twelve to fiftysomething. Miss Claudia was so much fun to watch because she was in her element — basking in the sun and thanking God for a beautiful day. Her happiness was contagious, and having my godmother with me was a gift.

After breakfast we set out in a big blue van to visit our first carepoint. The low-slung city buildings flowing by, then into neighborhoods, the nicer houses surrounded by barbed wire, the small houses coming next as we traveled up and down the hillsides. Eventually the road, going from asphalt down to dirt, afforded us views of even smaller houses and huts clinging to the green grass around them. We bumped farther into the countryside, the road narrowing even more until we reached the carepoint. According to Jumbo, this was the nicest carepoint, with its cinder block shed, books, and playthings.

As soon as we stepped out of the van, the children came running our way, their little bodies throbbing with excitement, the smaller ones raising their arms to be lifted up. Some were dressed in rags, others in older clothing inappropriate for the summer heat — fleece pullovers or long-sleeved shirts. One boy, a fantastic soccer player, wore a pink tank top with butterflies spread across its surface. The children there were so full of verve I wondered how they could have such terrible lives and still be this joyful.

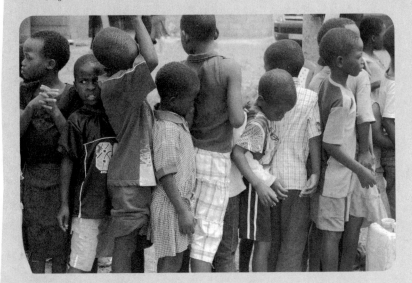

These kids lacked my sense of personal space as they stood in line to get lunch, their bodies pressed belly to back. Watching them eat what very likely was the only meal most would get that day filled my own stomach with sadness. But they sat around the carepoint, chatting as they scooped up the pap (a corn substance much like grits) and red beans with their fingers.

After they finished eating, all of them, down to the tiniest child, took their plates to the wash bin and cleaned off their dishes. Nobody complained. They squatted in front of the dishpan and rubbed their bowls clean of the food remains.

Jumbo brought out a moon bounce, an inflatable castle meant to turn kids into kangaroos. As it was inflating, the kids, freshly fed, jumped up and down in anticipation. Finally the castle was ready, and again, they stood in line, right against each other, waiting their turn, while, two at a time, they bounced their way across the surface. Their laughter echoed around the carepoint, and they didn't know whether to get back in line or join in the soccer game. Their energy remained until the last of the kids jumped their way to the slide.

Some of the older girls danced, inviting us to circle with them, each of us taking our turn dancing in the middle. They clapped to a bright rhythm, the group calling to the dancer in the middle. "I want to dance with you ..." And they laughed and pushed us inside, and we danced and danced, the entire circle moving inward at times. I felt like I was back on the playground in elementary school. All we were missing was the jump ropes. It was easy to tell who in our group had rhythm and who didn't. (Sorry, Mom.) But that didn't stop the girls from wanting us to try, their laughter resounding, their voices echoing over the countryside, their smiles broad and welcoming.

On the way to the carepoint, we were warned to take pictures only after asking for and receiving permission. A lot of ministries and aid organizations have taken advantage of the Swazis, snapping their pictures for fund-raising purposes but doing nothing to help.

But the kids that day loved having their photos taken. "Shoot! Shoot me!" they yelled, and we were happy to comply. After taking their photos, we showed them the picture on the screen, and they burst out laughing.

A beautiful little girl, her black hair streaked with blonde, came to sit on my lap. Tom said, "You see the blonde? That's from malnutrition." I hugged her close.

Some of these children walk for three miles to come for this meal, and what they go home to is anybody's guess. A mother dying in the back room? An uncle forcing himself on her in return for a loaf of bread she can take back to her family? It was something I could barely think about as we tried to just have fun with them. If I had allowed my mind to dwell on their situations, I would have followed them home that day. Sometimes I wonder why I didn't.

17

⌒⌒⌒⌒

BREAD OF LIFE

Pastor Walter is an ebullient Swazi man who lives in a small house near one of his carepoints. Walter smiles easily and will sweep a wide hand over his beloved countryside, laying out his hopes and dreams for the people he loves so beautifully and so well.

But before he established these places of hope and nourishment, Pastor Walter had been a little old-school in his approach to shepherding his church. He talked to them a lot. Then he realized his people "needed a lot more from me than words."

"AIDS in my community has made life brutal," he said, his eyes weary. "As a pastor I did a lot of funerals, and that's where my heart got so caught up—because when I bury a man, I know that his children are orphans and that we've got to take care of them as well."

"All this time I was preaching," Pastor Walter said, sitting in the rudimentary church, the hot wind blowing through the open windows, "and the number of orphans kept increasing, and the number of widows kept increasing."

Now Pastor Walter was doing more than talking.

Leaving Ty behind with the children at the bouncy castle, we arrived at the carepoint several kilometers outside Manzini to find Walter's own children washing laundry, stomp-stomping on clothes in a brightly colored plastic tub. Women sat on the steps near the compound's kitchen, chatting in the shade, waiting until it was time to cook the day's food. The sun boiled overhead.

He swept an arm in front of a new two-room building. "This is where we will start school this year. In just a few days."

"How many students?" I asked.

"About sixty." He smiled.

I looked into the window, two rooms the size of a child's bedroom. "In those rooms?"

He laughed. "The children, they're little."

The mind is important to this man as well. School in Swaziland isn't free. Say what you will about public education in the U.S. these days, but at least children who can't afford an education in a private Christian or preparatory school or whose parents choose not to send them to these institutions have someplace to go. Not so in Swaziland. Each child must pay a fee. Orphans can go for free, but they have to provide a death certificate—and this is a lot harder than it sounds. Sometimes a parent leaves the country and dies while away from home. Sometimes a parent leaves the country, period, with no word of where they've gone.

At one point, Pastor Walter gave away his own children's school fees to another family. I don't know if I could do that. In fact, I know I couldn't. I don't even begin to understand that kind of sacrifice, that mode of living where, truly, others come first.

I'm sad that his children couldn't go to school, and it doesn't make sense to me. Are you really supposed to give away your basic necessities? His children are beautiful, by the way. They stomped away on the family clothing, working out the dust and the dirt as we stood in front of the school God provided. God gave back to Walter far more than Walter gave. Now there's a school in Pastor Walter's front yard where his children attend, as well as other children who can't afford the government school.

That kind of trusting faith amazes me, and I cry out to experience such overwhelming trust in God. But not too loudly, I admit. What if God actually took me up on it? What would happen then?

Lord, I believe. Help my unbelief.

I once had a conversation with the associate pastor of a megachurch in the Midwest. The church had recently built a new state-of-the-art facility, spending more than one million dollars on the sound system alone. I'm always looking for good reasons to do things—one reason I'm called the Queen of Rationalization. If you want to find a reason to do something —almost anything, really—I can help you find one. At the time I told myself, "I'm sure they have a good reason for spending so much on a sound system, but for the life of me I can't imagine what it is."

Pastor Walter has no time for rationalizing, however. He's got people to feed. He escorted us to a field behind the church, green and gorgeous, stalks of corn shivering in the breeze blowing off the hills. His yellow shirt blazed in front of the cool green stalks. Pastor Walter was delighted at this accomplishment.

Pastors in Swaziland don't have the luxury of worrying about "saving souls"—instead they worry about keeping hungry, undernourished, and disease-wracked bodies alive for another day, another week. Pastor Walter's field of corn was a church building project worth supporting.

My faith changed when I understood that God wanted me to love others in his name, and that loving others meant meeting them and serving them. The difference between who I was—a person of ideas and doctrine—and who I wanted to be—a person of love and action—was never illustrated so clearly as on our first day in Swaziland.

But we weren't done yet.

Dennis, our missionary guide on the ground in Swaziland, piled us into his van, and we headed back down the dirt road. When I asked about his life as a missionary, he downplayed his career choice. "What else could I be doing? I could never be sitting in an office. I'd go crazy working for Best Buy!"

Who wouldn't?

Besides me, I mean. Me who spent the better part of the last two decades sitting on my couch writing books about people with lives more exciting than my own.

Dennis drives his beat-up van from village to village, honking and waving and yelling to Swazi children. Who knew such little acts, when done consistently, can make a big difference? For Dennis, expending himself means simply letting other people know he thinks it's great they were born. Dennis embodies Mother Teresa's assertion that "in this life we cannot do great things. We can only do small things with great love."

Our first day in Manzini, Dennis took us to Nazarene Hospital to visit the daughter of a pastor he knew. A strawberry blond, Dennis is a big, jeans-wearing guy with a face that looks happy even when he isn't smiling. We headed into the women's ward, and I was the one who felt entirely out of place. And entirely white. (All Caucasians should travel to a place—in another church, another town, or another country—where they are the only white person present. This is the kind of cognitive dissonance that changes people for the better, and the place in which God delights in leading those who are willing to follow him.)

Nazarene Hospital in Manzini, Swaziland's largest city (population: 110,500), was founded by a Scottish couple in the 1920s. This is health care at its best in Swaziland. In all honesty, we wouldn't send our family dog to a vet in Lexington with similar conditions.

In Swaziland, nobody *really* has AIDS; nobody seems to die from the disease. Swazis are in a state of near-total denial when it comes to AIDS. The disease is more accepted in the West, and we have the gay community to thank for that. Dying in obscurity while your family and doctors lie about the disease that's killing you is neither just nor merciful. But an insidious fear has created unspoken rules about who can die of what. Does shame have anything to do with it? Perhaps.

Shame isn't always bad; without it, and the recognition of our failures, we cannot confess and change. And that's a bigger shame. One of the reasons Jesus came was so we could own up to our sins. But the shame in Swaziland over AIDS only hurts the victims.

The buildings of Nazarene Hospital are painted yellow ocher with maroon trim, and the concrete paths of the breezeways connecting its several buildings are polished to a light sheen by the shuffling of many feet. I felt like I was in a movie made in the fifties, in which Katherine Hepburn, playing a famous doctor with a heart for Africa, would round the corner ready to tell some official a thing or two about mercy and true humanity.

Dennis could play that sort of role, if push came to shove, I suppose.

If everybody lived life like Dennis does, world poverty would be nonexistent because we'd all make sure there was enough food to go around. And doing so wouldn't be a big pain or a cause for pride; it would simply be the natural outcome of a pure heart. Blessed are the pure in heart, and blessed are those the pure in heart befriend.

Dennis's yellow T-shirt blared the words *Dignity Justice Respect* in electric blue across his broad back. A Teamsters T-shirt. Dennis is from a blue-collar area of upstate New York. (Not every Christian in the world thinks unions are of the Devil. If you're hyperventilating right now, just hold a paper bag over your mouth and nose and breathe in and out; you'll be OK.)

We were at the hospital because Dennis had interrupted our tour of Pastor Walter's second church to have us visit a family down the hill. Multicolored hens and roosters bobbed around the dirt yard pecking for food. Inside, we found that their little boy was suffering from a painfully swollen eye. Dennis canceled his other plans. "You want to see what we do? Well, this is it, ladies."

We waited while the family put on their Sunday clothes—mother wearing a full skirt and a hat, her son in a clean plaid shirt and shorts. We squeezed into the van and headed back into Manzini.

While the little boy and his mother waited in the sweltering admitting room, sitting together on a bench near a counter, Dennis ushered us through the outdoor labyrinth of passageways and buildings, past some folks on gurneys waiting in the open air outside the X-ray room or the lab and past other patients strolling on the sidewalks with their IV poles in hand.

We entered the women's ward to visit Dennis's friend.

I didn't do a head count like the deacon at the back of the church on Sunday morning—honestly, who wants to count sick and dying people?

The long room was divided up into three sections. The large windows let in a bit of air, but no air-conditioning cooled the summer day. And yet, many of the patients lay bundled up in blankets, the sun filtering through the trees to cast dappled light on their beds.

That's when the audacity of what I had done by coming here hit me: I was an American woman who, at the age of forty, suddenly realized that God talked about his beloved poor and oppressed *all the time* in Scripture (see the appendix in the back of this book), saying that helping them was not an option for followers of Jesus who wanted to enter into his kingdom.

So here I was, ready to save the day! I wanted to slap myself. What was I supposed to do here? Wave? Pat the patients' legs as I strolled by their beds? Recite just the right Bible verse? I stuck out like a healthy thumb between row upon row of bedsores, lesions, and wasted bodies. What in God's name was I playing at?

I followed Dennis down the center aisle. I looked people in the eye and gave a little smile, a respectful nod. It was the best I could do. I was intruding in this hospital; I was intruding in this country.

Flies buzzed around the room. Family members congregated around some of the beds, while other patients lay in solitude. I smelled the sweet-sour odor of bodily fluids and motionless figures. We were all sweating as we walked past bed after bed after bed and were finally introduced to the people we'd come to visit. As I took a seat, commotion charged the middle of the room when a group of people filed in, dressed in their good clothes, looking quite handsome. The woman in the bed across from us sat up, breasts bare, to see what was going on. The guests congregated in a cluster in the middle of the room and began singing hymns. I couldn't figure out the words, but I knew the tune — "Leaning on the Everlasting Arms." If you've never heard Africans singing to God, you've never heard the pinnacle of praise on earth.

The visitors were folks from a church who wanted to bless the sick and the dying, those imprisoned by their circumstances, their illness, their soon-coming death to a disease nobody could fix for good. The visitors came to give a cup of cold water to the women, to sit with the lonely. These were Matthew 25 people!

When the singing stopped, a tall, fine-looking man dressed in pressed pants and an immaculate white shirt with a dark tie opened his Bible. The shouting began, the preaching, and I wished I could understand what he was saying. The skeptic in me (oh, I can be a skeptic!) figured he was yelling at people for not "being saved." That he was telling them they'd better "get right with God" before they "passed into eternity." This was their big chance to stay out of hell. (As if they weren't in it already.) "Jesus could come tonight! Stop living your lives of sin!"

What was he saying? I don't know. I brought my own biases to the table and couldn't discern the truth of the situation. But I saw the eyes of the patients begin to look down, then to glaze. Some rolled over in their beds, encasing their shoulders and necks in their blankets, and closed their eyes. A few minutes later, family members went back to their chit-chat with those they came to see and care for.

Sometimes the Good News can sound like such bad news, can't it?

The church members finished up with another song, then filed around the ward shaking the hands of the patients. This took five minutes, and they were gone.

Who am I to judge?

What had those church members already been through in their own lives? Surely they'd lost loved ones to HIV/AIDS and tuberculosis. Perhaps the women had husbands who'd deserted them, went off on forays into the city, and left them to care for the children on their own—for years and years—only to return and pass on HIV and expect their wives to care for them as they died from the very disease they'd given their family.

Who am I to judge? What was I doing for anybody in that room?

I needed to sit back and shut up and let God teach me. Sometimes I want to know it all, be it all, give it all, and have it all, but most times God just wants me to sit still and let him speak.

I turned back to the people we'd come to visit.

The Swazi lady—dressed European-style in a black skirt and an overshirt of burgundy and black, hair tucked beneath a black straw hat—sat in a straight chair by her daughter's bed in the far right corner of the room. Dennis greeted her, and we all shook hands in the Swazi manner, touching our left hand to our right forearm as a sign of respect, bowing a little as our right hands grasped and shook once.

The daughter, in her late teens according to Dennis, lay on her side, listless. The whites of her eyes were large and yellowish, the life-light in the brown of her irises an anemic reflection of what it must have been when she was a little girl running around her homestead. The sight of this dying girl—a teenager who should be in the prime of her life—produced strong emotions. AIDS had given this young woman the body of an eighty-year-old. There her precious mother sat, mourning, likely knowing her daughter had AIDS but too frightened to admit it.

Let me challenge you: When you picture this woman sitting by her daughter's deathbed—day after sweltering day, week after claustrophobic week, month after wasting month—think of your own child, or your sister or brother. Understand that the only thing you can do is watch death arrive. Do you feel the stabbing helplessness lancing straight to the softest middle of your heart? Do you wonder who will be next? Do you wish it was you?

When Dennis asked that mother what we could do to help, she said, "Please pray." When Claudia asked what Americans could do to help the people of Swaziland, she said once again, "We need them to pray for us."

It's easy for me, surrounded by so many people who do wonderful works of mercy and compassion, to forget about prayer. But suffering people seem to remember, in the midst of their pain and their loneliness, that *God hears the cry of his people.* God hears the cry of the poor, and those cries—and ours—make a difference.

If he doesn't, let's turn out the lights and go home.

I once heard a Christian woman talk about AIDS in Africa and say, "Well, it's their own fault. They're sexually promiscuous. God's just letting nature take its course. If I help, I'm just allowing sin to prosper."

I didn't know what to say to her. I still don't.

Then I noticed an old woman who lay dying, curled up like a discarded paper bag. The human body is inexplicably, horribly resilient. The little remaining flesh on her face was pulled tightly across the protruding bones of her skull, and her receding gums made her yellow teeth appear long and canine. Her calves and feet stuck out from underneath her blanket; my thumb and middle finger could have touched in a loop around her ankle.

Claudia and Andrea stepped to either side of the woman's bed. I watched as they helped the woman to a sitting position, an effort that required minutes of gentle pushing and lifting. The old woman hadn't yet eaten her breakfast that was sitting on a tray on a bedside table; it was about three in the afternoon. Nobody feeds you at the hospitals in Swaziland; that's what your family is for. If your family abandons you, you are as good as dead.

I watched as the old woman labored to remain sitting, her body convulsing with the effort. Claudia held the woman's head upright, her fingers cupped around the back of her skull, supporting her as a mother would an infant. Andrea lifted a cup and a plate from the bedside table. The toast was crawling with ants; a line of the insects rimmed the edge of the cup of orange juice. The women flicked them off and began breaking off small bits of toast. I watched bread and juice placed in the mouth of a dying woman, served by women dying a bit more slowly.

I watched the hands of Jesus—flicking ants, breaking bread—even as I clenched my own.

I once stood in an AIDS ward in a hospital in Swaziland, watching the hands of Jesus touch the withered bodies of his children, his diseased and dying children.

I am fortunate to have seen that AIDS ward because I know this: Jesus lives in the city of Manzini, in a sweltering ocher room. In my prayers I go back there and sit alongside a hard hospital bed. In my prayers I see Jesus, breaking stale, insect-covered bread, expending himself in love.

18

PEOPLE OF THE BOOK

Sunday, our second full day in Swaziland, dawned with an overcast sky that seemed to draw the heat up from the earth and throw it back down again, right on top of our heads. Claudia, Christy, and I woke up early, dressed in our modest skirts and shirts, and set out, the concrete sidewalks of Manzini still abandoned, to the cathedral for early Mass. One-quarter of Swazis are Catholic Christians, while one-third are Protestant Christians. Another third are African-Zionist, a blend between Christianity and indigenous ancestral worship, while Mormonism, Judaism, the Bahá'í Faith, Islam, and other religions account for the last 15 percent or so. In the widely practiced ancestral religion, witch doctors hold a great deal of sway over their people through fear and superstition.

The Wesleyans got the Christian party started, and the legend of how it happened—everybody assures me it's true—sounds like the sort of thing God might do.

King Sobhuza, who ruled Swaziland from 1805–39, had a dream. A stranger with pale skin and "hair like a cow tail" held out his hands. In one hand he clutched a book, in the other a coin purse. In the dream, the king was instructed to take the book. He didn't live to see the dream fulfilled in his lifetime, but his son Mswati did when missionaries arrived. Christianity was brought into Swaziland and accepted. Unfortunately, King Mswati also accepted the money bag. That part didn't turn out so well.

That first Sunday in Swaziland testified to the global beat of God's heart. We entered the bright cathedral, having trekked up the walkway lined with flowers, opened one of the tall double doors, and stood for a moment at the back beneath the soaring ceiling, the stations of the cross lined up on the walls beside us. We were handed a bulletin and took our seat with the other twenty or so people attending Mass. It was to be said in siSwati, the language of Swaziland. Listening to Mass in another language, quite frankly, thrilled me. I knew *Dios* was God and *Christos* meant Christ; I could tell when the "Our Father" was being said, as well as the "Holy, Holy, Holy."

I couldn't speak with my brothers and sisters, but I could know — and I did know because I was captured in this one moment in time when I could not think of the future of this city — this country in which I found myself. I was captured by the now, by the liturgy I knew so well. I stepped with them along the path, as we'd done together, week by week, year by year, century by century — that path never changing as it took us to God, the one who became man and took on our infirmities, our sicknesses, our frailties, even the very sins that took us down to our graves. It was here, in this celebration, that we cast aside our own plans and placed them at the foot of the cross — our jobs, our health, our families. It was here that we laid our concerns on the altar, our prayers for our people, believing by faith Christ would enter in as he did two thousand years ago, and as he does every time the Eucharist is offered.

With these precious people, we celebrated at the same table as our brothers and sisters all over the world, past, present, and future. When I realized how we were all one in the Spirit that day, unified by our faith in God, I cried. No Jew or Greek, male or female, Swazi or American.

I looked around the cathedral and wondered how many of the worshipers would die in the next year, or the next month. How many would be worshiping here if I came back to visit? *Lamb of God, you take away the sins of the world; have mercy on us. Lamb of God, you take away the sins of the world; grant us peace.*

WORSHIP IN A WEARY LAND

Ty

Mom woke me up when she returned from Mass. It was time to get ready to attend Pastor Walter's church. When we all arrived, the younger kids were scattered beneath a shade tree like fruit, listening to Swagheli, a vibrant young Swazi woman wearing a colorful dress and a bright smile, teach them about Jesus. The heat of the day had already begun to infuse the air, and I figured that the kids had the best deal, since we bigger folks were going to head inside the muggy building soon for a multihour service. When the kids' lesson ended, their teacher began singing and clapping, and all the kids started to dance for Jesus in a circle with such life and joy that I couldn't take my eyes away. Much like the circle of girls at the carepoint the day before, they clapped and swayed, moving their bodies freely and without a hint of care. It was like watching the Holy Spirit in motion as these children in a nation of dying people danced before their Savior.

We filed inside. I sat next to Mom and waited for church to begin. The tiny church with a concrete floor was separated by gender — the men on the right, the women on the left. We sang for what seemed like an eternity, hymn after hymn, a cappella and filled with harmony — and it was so holy that I never wanted it to stop. Listening to the voices, strong and hitting the notes with perfect pitch, I felt like I got a little taste of heaven on that hot summer day, and what normally would have caused me to keep checking the time flew past me until I realized we had been singing for at least an hour.

As the first hour of singing ended, Pastor Walter got up to speak. Both his gap-toothed smile and energetic demeanor

immediately put me at ease. He's such a happy man, yet his topic was serious. He talked about the AIDS epidemic in Swaziland and how the men there were "dropping like flies."

Dropping like flies. Can you imagine hearing this from the front of your church? Can you imagine having to say this about the people of your country? Some of these people are his friends, his peers, his family—and they are dying. His nation is rapidly becoming extinct. I wouldn't know what to do if the people around me started dying off—and not just friends and family of "other people," but Gwynnie, Jake, Mom, and Dad. I fear I would throw up my hands—or worse—against such odds.

Pastor Walter has been sent by God to help his people, and so he does. His school and his carepoints make the love of Jesus tangible every day. Knowing God will provide — knowing because he sees it happen time and time again — he gives people money from his own pocket, even though he can't afford it. I was amazed at how passionate he was about helping the people around him, including even perfect strangers as if they were his own family. Although he is surrounded by pain, Pastor Walter knows the joy of drawing near to his God. Why pain and nearness to God go hand in hand, I can't understand. I wish it weren't so.

And if I'm honest, I share something in common with Pastor Walter. I, too, have been challenged by God to help people. And so I try. More and more as the years go by, as I meet more and more of God's needy children who are crying out for justice, love, and a savior.

I have so far to go, but I can already look back and see the place from which God called me. It was a place of comfort and insulation. A place with little pain and little nearness to God. Watching Pastor Walter was like reading a living, breathing manual of how it's done.

The church service continued on African time with singing, dancing, and testimony. (Americans wouldn't put up with a three-hour service for even one week — we have to get to our favorite restaurant before the noon rush or jump back into our pj's to read the Sunday paper!) Our group had to leave early; yet when we piled in the van, the service had been going for almost three hours. We waved to our African brothers and sisters in Christ; united by the Holy Spirit, our world is the biggest smallest family imaginable.

19

RABBITS AND CATFISH

But Sunday wasn't over yet. Grabbing some Kentucky Fried Chicken wraps (yes, we left Kentucky only to get KFC in Swaziland), we ate in the van as we traveled up the country's major highway to see what was being done elsewhere for orphans and to meet Kevin Ward, a man with a heart for children, a soul for God, and a head for administration.

Kevin Ward grew up as what is known as a "white Swazi," numbered among the few Caucasians born there. We arrived at his farm, Hwane, having driven through Mbabane (*Buh-bahn*) — the capital of Swaziland about twenty kilometers from Manzini — and into a higher elevation. The green-sloped mountains near Piggs Peak, another twenty-five or so kilometers from Mbabane, did little to quell the heat, however, and as we stood outside his complex waiting for their church service to end, I sought but didn't find much shade. Already, this fair-skinned woman was beginning to broil. My hat didn't feel like it was doing a thing.

Kevin was raised in privilege. His father owns the Mountain Inn, one of Swaziland's only resorts. It's the place to go if you can afford it. The view from the pool is worth six months' pay — which is probably what it would cost the typical inhabitant of Mbabane to stay for one night.

Kevin is truly a Swazi in another way. He loves the people of his country and works to better their situation. It wasn't enough for him to provide luxurious lodging for tourists and the wealthier inhabitants. Kevin chose to provide lodging of another kind, utilizing his business mind and organizational skills to make life better for the orphans in his country. God bless him. Obviously his heart is as big as his intellect. It would take a lot of love to leave behind a place as gorgeous as the Mountain Inn.

The compound at Kevin's Hwane Farm consists of a church, dormitories, classrooms, an infirmary, a fish hatchery, and a rabbit shed where they raise their own meat. The buildings sit far apart, with grassy spaces in between, and the place possesses a spacious air, unhurried but sturdy. Gardens grow near the small water treatment building, and a quiet calm soaked us in its depths.

Kevin began the tour outside on the lawn, his clothing pressed and neat despite the heat, his salt-and-pepper hair combed back from his forehead. We stood in a circle around him, trying to catch every word from his soft-spoken tongue.

"Protein is important when trying to turn sick children into healthy ones," Kevin said, explaining the ratios of the diet consumed by the orphans. "So we grow a lot of our own meat. You'll see as we progress."

Organic, sustainable farming. Kevin is a man of vision on more than one level. He'd probably love what's going on at the London Ferrell Community Garden.

He turned and walked down a path toward two buildings up ahead. The dormitories.

How different it is to be a pastor in Swaziland than in America! So much time and effort is spent on food—planting, growing, reaping, storing, distributing, stretching, collecting. In Swaziland, the gospel isn't a formula for daily living or a ticket out of hell; it's literally served in a bowl, grown in a field, and hooked from a pond. Ministry is hands-on because if it isn't, people die. The luxury of separating the "spiritual" from the "physical" is unimaginable. Commitment to the call of Christ is something you can taste and see, something you can plant and water.

As Kevin led us through the dormitories, he explained that many of the children arrived HIV positive, that somehow—with love, respect, strength of purpose, and proper nutrition—many of them, with stronger bodies and cared-for hearts, never developed full-blown AIDS. Miracles do happen.

I jammed my hat further down on my head, thankful for the cool skirts we wore. Before we came to Swaziland, we were told not to wear pants—only prostitutes did that. Ty and I went to the bargain table at JoAnne's and picked out some fabric, and our friend Alana sewed it into skirts long enough to not be considered immodest. I still wear them. They're kinda cute.

But as we stood in the yard, Kevin said, "We have our girls wear pants. It's less likely they'll be raped that way. I realize it goes against the culture, but their safety is more important."

My jaw dropped. Rape is a frequent occurrence in Swaziland, where women are treated with less respect than we'd treat a stray cat. Women have no place of honor and are treated as objects, expected to do the work without question or receiving thanks. If a man wants a Swazi girl, it's his right to have her.

Girls are raped repeatedly by their uncles, fathers, brothers, and the man next door. And according to Kevin, there's only one bona fide psychologist in all of Swaziland. When I think of all the universities and colleges and seminaries in the United States that are pumping out more master's degrees in counseling than the church in America can possibly need, I pray some of them will end up in Africa, helping to heal girls who have been raped and traumatized.

My Gwynnie is eleven. She goes to sleepovers, rehearses for her school plays (she can do a killer British accent), and cares for the brood of chicks we just bought—and I don't have to consider the possibility that she'll be raped when she gets dressed in the morning.

Are you getting a counseling degree? Just thought I'd ask.

I AM HOPING

Ty

When I turned eighteen, I got my first tattoo. Inked on my left shoulder blade is the Hebrew word for hope. Translated, it actually means, "I am hoping." So much about who I want to be, how I long to respond, who I view God to be is tied up in that word.

Kevin Ward is the human representation of my tattoo, a man full of hope and longing for the coming of God's Kingdom. My mom has told you a little bit about his compound, but the tour isn't over.

Kevin also has programs for people dealing with alcohol and drug addictions, but what we were most interested in was his program for orphans. On his farm, Kevin houses eight kids in a dormitory home with a Swazi caregiver. By the time an orphan is four, he or she has a personal garden on the self-sustainable farm. Along with the gardens, the orphans raise cattle, catfish, and rabbits. According to Kevin, having living plants and animals to be responsible for is an important part of the healing process most Swazi orphans must go through. Most of them—boys as well as girls—have been abused. No law exists against abusing boys, and oftentimes the sexual abuse of male children is overlooked. Hwane Farm keeps a counselor on staff for the kids to talk to and to receive therapy from.

On the other side of the dormitories, there's an infirmary for the children living with HIV/AIDS. This wing is brightly colored in sherbet shades of pinks, greens, blues, and yellows. It is, as much as possible, a cheerful place—a place for children to die happily. Thankfully, during our visit, no children inhabited the space, but I couldn't help but picture little bodies beneath the sheets. We are all born to die, but so soon? God, have mercy.

Somehow, in spite of the abundant reasons to despair, Kevin wakes up with a feeling of hope—at least most days. He believes he is raising the next leaders of Swaziland, and he's probably right. Since there is schooling and skill training at Hwane, the kids who survive will leave with a better chance for productive employment than most, and some will no doubt become leaders of their communities.

Jobs are scarce in Swaziland. Many of the men don't work; many of those who do are serving as migrant laborers in South Africa. While away, many contract HIV/AIDS, come back into Swaziland, and pass their disease, usually undiagnosed, to their wives. Kevin is tired of watching this cycle of death spin on and on. Many years ago, he decided to commit his life to protecting as many Swazi children as he could. He follows Jesus every day because he has to; on his own, he'd be lost and overwhelmed.

As I witnessed Swazi leaders like Kevin and Pastor Walter

exhibit such love to the people around them, sheltering them, protecting, healing, and listening, I realized I wouldn't have believed such dedication and obedience unless I'd seen it with my own eyes. I was overwhelmed by the desire to be like them, to visit the widows and the orphans in their distress. I decided that I wanted a reminder to be a loving person, so in March, I got my second tattoo. Inked in black on my wrist is the Greek word αγάπη ('agape' in English, pronounced ah-**gah**-pey). Agape means 'unconditional love' and was a word often used by Jesus. Underneath the inked word on my wrist is Saint Peter's cross — upside down, for he felt he was unworthy to be crucified in the same manner as his Lord. It reminds me to be humble.

My goal is that when I see this tattoo, I will be reminded of the work that these men and women do in Swaziland to truly help people. They do this work with a love and humility that can only be given by Christ. And I pray, hoping that one day Christ will make me a more loving person. But for now, I have my tattoos that help me remember God and his loving ways, his work in this broken world through people who share all they have and give of all they are. And I have hope in the God who transforms, making gold from dross and wine from water, and I pray he'll do the same for me.

20

HOPE AMID THE HELPLESS

It's easy to feel good about what Kevin Ward is doing. The innocent, victimized children at Hwane Farm are easy to love; it's in our nature to reach out to children. At times I've thought it would be great if the church could just concentrate on kids—we'd save the next generation and not waste our efforts on adults, who aren't likely to change anyway! I'm glad God isn't as jaded as I am.

Sexual promiscuity is the norm in Swaziland. One pastor shook his head and said his church focuses on people eighteen and younger, trying to give them an alternative, a way of respect for their bodies and the bodies of others. "It's just too late for the older people," he said sadly.

But Jesus wants his love in us to continually reach across our thresholds and away from our easy chairs. I can think of many a person in Scripture who didn't deserve the "hand up" the Son of God gave him or her. And it would be easy to lump together all those who have contracted AIDS through their own choices and call them "an issue" or "a problem." It's tempting to avoid actually categorizing them as human beings made in the image of God.

But this isn't a matter of belief or doctrine; it's an issue of friendship. Have you ever noticed how an opinionated person can change his or her tune about something when it comes down to the personal level? He can be completely against divorce, until his sister is struggling in an abusive marriage. She roundly condemns homosexuality as a perversion, something only the most wicked of people practice, until her son sits her down for the big talk.

Wandile (pronounced Wan-*dee*-lay) was a good friend of Dennis. We were driving down the highway, and I tapped out Dennis's words into my portable word processor as he recalled for us a flesh and blood woman who lived by her own code yet died in the arms of Jesus.

Wandile lived in Pastor Walter's community of Timbutini. She grew up there and lived a wild life as a crazy teenager — sleeping around, drinking, doing what she pleased — and she wanted nothing to do with God. Nothing unusual. We have plenty of those young people in our own country.

Wandile contracted AIDS, not surprisingly, and was OK for a while, going about her work, her life. Yet after a while, Dennis noticed that she was thinner, her once sturdy frame reducing a little each week, and each time he saw her, her feet shuffled along with more difficulty, slowing her pace, bowing her shoulders. Everyone knew she was sick and had HIV, but because of the stigma, she was viewed as a curse, shunned by neighbors and people she thought were friends, most likely playmates from childhood or women she once trusted with her secrets. Then the worst thing that could happen, did.

Wandile was kicked out of her house by her father, who had always seemed like a nice guy, but when faced with AIDS, he did what most people did — denied its existence by shoving it away. Her mother lived in South Africa — she'd moved away years before. And as always seems to be the case when you think it's darkest, the horizon deepened yet further when Wandile took a turn for the worse. Thank God for the ray of light he sent in Thembie, a single mom and a faithful friend of Wandile, also HIV positive, who brought Wandile into her house and took care of her.

Dennis tried to help Wandile get the ARVs (antiretrovirals) she needed, and some of the people from the ministry drove her around the city looking for help. She had originally tested positive at the government hospital far away, and Manzini Hospital told her to go back to that hospital and start the ARVs there. Red tape.

So Dennis, along with a friend and Wandile, drove eighty kilometers the next day to the place she was diagnosed. They waited for hours and tried to explain what happened and that she lived in Manzini — and it would be difficult to come for treatment so far away. She was given a transfer letter, but tough luck on the ARVs: "Go back to Manzini and get them there."

Dennis, discouraged and angry, took her by the arm, and they walked out. Parked near his old van sat a brand-new double-cab pickup truck emblazoned with the logo of a well-known American charity. "I thought of how all the money good people sent went to buy these brand-new trucks, but my friend had never seen a cent of this money," he said as we drove along the highway.

"Lisa, this is so symbolic of the struggle we face."

Back they traveled to Manzini for the ARVs. Nevertheless, before long, Wandile became bedridden, her legs weakened, her body slowing down. It was hard on Thembie, who was in no great shape herself. They asked the church for help, hoping some relief would come, but people didn't want to help Wandile. Or Thembie, for that matter.

"Maybe Thembie wasn't the best churchgoer," Dennis said. "But she was acting like Jesus to Wandile. She might have not been up to the church's moral standards, but she was doing the work."

I guess America isn't the only place where holiness is based more on what you don't do than on what you do.

Wandile's condition worsened. She was having trouble eating, and diarrhea wracked her thin body, dehydrating her. She lost more weight lying in her bed day after day, staring at the ceiling, alone more often than not. Despite all this, and even as she was shunned by the church, Wandile gave her life to Jesus in a quiet moment, realizing she needed God to enter her life, to lie down beside her, to love her right where she was. Sometimes Jesus steps in and does what his followers are too "holy" to do themselves.

Thembie had no running water or electricity, so caring for Wandile, cleaning her and bathing her with water from the well, became impossible. Finally Dennis took Wandile to Hope House. The ministry was founded to give free care, but when they arrived, they found out they were required to pay three hundred Rand a month as well as provide their own caregiver and food. So much for free care. Still, it was the only hope they had.

"We needed someone to attend her. Wandile was there for about a month, but then people lost interest in helping and we couldn't get care-givers. Not even a family member. Her mother said, 'My daughter is dead already. Call me when you have the funeral.' The family rejected her. In the end we had to take Wandile out of Hope House."

Wandile was utterly deserted by her church family and her biological family.

The ARVs and drugs gave Wandile paranoia and hallucinations. She was difficult at times, lashing out physically with fists and slaps and ver-bally with curses and howls. At times her words were downright bizarre.

"Dennis, I've been to see the Eskimos in Alaska."

She wouldn't eat for fear her food was poisoned, and the weight loss continued. So she went back to Thembie's house, in such poor condition that by then it seemed she was about to die. Ailing Thembie began caring for her again.

Adventures in Mission, Dennis's agency, had a first-year missionary team in Swaziland during that period. Joe, one of the missionaries, said, "We can't let her die. Let's fast and pray." So they did pray over her and fasted—people would sign up for different times and days. Joe's enthusi-asm spread over the team, and their faith burgeoned as they trusted God to hear them, to see Wandile and to step in and heal.

And then something began to happen over the next couple of months. She started to gain some weight and stopped being combative, and even-tually her mind returned. One day, she threw back her blanket, planted her feet on the floor, and stood up. She started walking again. And eating. Wandile came back to life and wanted to tell the world about it. She began testifying that she'd given her life to Christ, preaching to the young kids not to live like she did. She didn't want to see others suffer the way she had.

The Lord gave her a grace period in which she attended church and tried to help out. She lived for another year, back on her feet, walking around, looking like she was doing well and in her right mind. But still she needed a home. She didn't want to be a burden to Thembie anymore. So the team moved her to her aunt's place, an hour and a half away.

Away from the missionary team, Dennis, and the people who cared, Wandile got sick again, this time with tuberculosis, another widespread disease in Swaziland. Dennis drove her to Nazarene Hospital in Manzini. (Her bed was the same bed in which the pastor's daughter had lain dying.) Bedridden again, failing and wasting once more, Wandile's family deserted her again. Her father came once, but never again. Pastor Walter would visit when he was in town, doing his best to encourage her. Joe, whose ministry was visiting people in the hospital, would visit almost every day. She would beg everyone, "Please get me out of here."

And who could blame her in that place where flies infest food, and no one feeds it to you even if it's there? Who could blame her in that blazing-hot room with little air circulating? Who could blame her, continually breathing in death?

Dennis's eyes filled with tears as he continued the story. "During Wandile's last days we tried to organize a place for her to go, but no one would take her. She died alone in that disgusting place. I saved a message on my phone—her last message—asking for someone to take her away.

"I was away in South Africa when she died, and no one had seen her. The last time I had seen her, she grabbed my hand and said, 'Don't let me die here.' I told her to hang on."

No one had seen Wandile for the forty-eight hours before she died.

"I wish I would have checked on her more. But I have so much to do. I wish I would have made a lot more time to be with her at the hospital."

Dennis's words pulled down my stomach with grief and sadness. It's easy to judge the church people and the family; but I have to be careful there because I wasn't around for Wandile, let alone for the people dying of AIDS here in Lexington.

Sometimes we can mistake our opinions of others for action. We feel right, and that's enough. It's a comfortable trap.

What grieves me most is that Dennis, who's truly on the front lines and in need of an extra ten hours a day to fulfill his responsibilities, might live with a misplaced guilt for the rest of his life. I pray he doesn't do so. He's too good a person, too caring a soul, too much like Jesus in a land where people die alone as they leave desperate messages asking for someone to come and take them home.

People will say that Wandile was wild, that she brought her suffering on herself.

Let's put that aside for a moment. What about the children who lose a mother or father to AIDS? How is AIDS affecting them? Can we help the parents, despite their sexual misconduct, in order to keep a home together? Swaziland doesn't need any more orphans. Must children suffer to teach their parents a lesson?

Lord, have mercy on us if we think that's the holiness God calls his children to practice. Lord, have mercy on us if we believe it's our job to decide who God is punishing and who he isn't. Lord, have mercy on us if we believe dying alone, emaciated and wracked with emotional and physical pain, is a fitting end for any of God's children.

21

SCHOOLHOUSE ROCK

The next morning, the writers group piled back into the blue van with Dennis and Tom, still set on our mission of meeting the people of Swaziland, the pastors, the servants, the sick, the children, anyone we could, so that we could spread the word to the church back home that God needed us there.

After another breakfast on the patio of our hotel, we slid into our modest skirts once again, grabbed water bottles and our cameras, and headed out. We whizzed down the highway, Dennis honking at the kids walking to school, passing little markets and people selling produce in stalls. He pulled off the main road, and we bumped along to the home of Pastor Sam and his wife, Happiness — I know, isn't that the greatest name ever? At the time, I didn't realize how important this day would become in my life, how God would plant a piece of my affection with his servant.

They ushered us with Swazi graciousness into their small home — just two rooms, a small kitchen, and a bathroom. The living room also housed the bunk beds of their two daughters. Inspirational art was tacked up on the walls, and books abounded. We piled into the room, the girls hopping up onto the top bunk and passing down stuffed animals to show Ty, who immediately began making them talk.

We liked Sam right away. Swazi men are more reserved toward women than men are in the U.S., but his obvious affection for his wife and daughters and the way he talked directly to the women in the group instead of ignoring us—as we were beginning to get used to—made us feel more at home. They told us of their dream to build a church that would help their country folk live and grow and love in the name of Jesus.

We piled back into the van again as Sam led us to an abandoned, condemned house. Behind the crumbling porch the empty rooms begged to be filled with the children who once went to school there, children Sam and his flock were educating who couldn't afford the fees for the government schools. "We were meeting there before summer, but now we can no longer." Summer break was ending in two days. "We don't know what we're going to do."

The house looked ready to implode, but children had come there anyway, an education one of their only hopes for avoiding a life of poverty, starvation, and sickness.

Sam turned, and we walked fifty or so yards through a patch of grass bordered on the left by woods and scrub that opened onto a field. The warm breeze dried a little of the sweat from the already blazing heat of the morning. He swept his hand over the gently sloping expanse. "I need to feed my people," he said. "We hope to grow corn here. But we need a fence first."

Next Pastor Sam took us through the village of Mangwaneni, where mud houses are stacked like shoeboxes up a crumbling, red hillside. A winding path led up the hill, where the hot sun baked an unfinished steel structure. I thought about how nimbly I could run through the woods when I was young, but in the village, I felt like a lumbering, uncoordinated she-bear. The entire ascent I was thinking, *If it's this hard going up, I'm going to fall flat on my face coming down!*

It wasn't but a few seconds after we arrived that children began to follow us, laughing at our white skin and at some of the yellow heads among us, Ty's included. One boy kept pointing to me and doubling over in delight. I decided I'd laugh right along with him, like I might do if a group of purple people came into the Third Street Coffee Shop in Lexington.

Soon a girl attached herself to me. Her name was Nothando. Thick, curly lashes rimmed her eyes, and her thin frame moved gracefully. She followed me around with no suspicion, and as she walked beside me, she put her hand in mine, or clung to my arm. I just wanted to paste her to my side and never let go.

We approached the home of a woman who lived with her mother and cared for five children, four of them not her own. The foster care system in Swaziland is both self-run and absolutely essential. Orphans don't find themselves wards of the state; they find themselves wards of their aunts, their grandmothers, or their neighbors. And when those connections break down, they find themselves wards of each other.

We entered her two-room home and passed through the first room—a lean-to. The second room, about ten by twelve, held a table and a bed a bit wider than a single bed, made up neatly with a rough, gray wool blanket.

Imagine you are that woman, but you lived in the United States. How would it make you feel if someone brought a group of people to your home to show them how poor you are? There you are, living in the "bad section" of your town, scraping by, knowing people think you've got to be at least somewhat at fault, somewhat complicit in your circumstances, even though you're taking care of three of your nieces and nephews, your little brother, and your own kids, whose dad left them four years before. You want to work, for goodness' sake. But there's no job nearby, and three of those kids are under the age of four. How are you going to pay for their child care?

And yet this Swazi woman met us with graciousness, even going so far as to let the food she was cooking in the lean-to burn because it would be rude to leave one's guests—and she didn't have much food to burn. Swazi manners are far more genteel than ours. Pastor Sam explained who we were, and the woman smiled and looked down at the ground a lot. Her few possessions she kept tidy.

I wondered how she went along day after day in the dim recesses of her house. Did the children's laughter as they ran up and down the paths make it bearable? Did she ever get together with the other women of the village and talk about all the things we talk about—our hair, our men, our thighs? I never had the chance to ask, because we soon moved on to another house, where a young man nodded and talked in siSwati with Pastor Sam, who was checking on his welfare.

After that we climbed to the top of the hill, over rocks and up a skinny path that I suspected only goats should be able to climb, toward a steel structure. We walked inside the structure; only supports held up a steel roof. The floor was nonexistent except as God made it, with a pile of gravel in the middle.

This roof and these supports were adequate—but without enough money to make a school out of it, the structure sat empty. I asked how much it would take to finish the building.

"Between twelve and fourteen thousand American dollars," Pastor Sam said. Obviously he had been thinking about this for a while.

Maybe the upper school could meet there, I thought. I pictured them in school uniforms, heading to class with books under their arms, learning history and math, raising their hands to answer questions with a wave that signaled the teacher to "Pick me! Pick me!" And then, breaking for lunch, congregating after school to gossip—kids offered opportunities to build a new life, a better future.

On the way back to the van, Tom and Dennis presented the elder of the village with a sack of groceries and gave a bag of food to the dear woman whose lunch had burned because of our visit.

The most thrilling part of the trip was watching Tom and Dennis see a need, hop in the van, and come back with bags of groceries—boom, need met! How much different would my life be if I ran my actions through fewer filters? Can you imagine Jesus being asked to heal and responding, "Oh, I was on my way to the synagogue. I'll catch you when I'm finished, and we'll take care of that disease then." What would it look like if I lived in imitation of the Father, who owns the cattle on a thousand hills and says his mercies are from everlasting to everlasting?

As we stood waiting for Tom and Dennis to finish distributing the food, Andrea pulled out some bubbles. Amid the iridescent glow of the floating orbs, a couple of girls decided to give us Swazi names. Ty became Nokukhanoya, meaning "a lady of brightness," and Nothando proclaimed me Tengetile, which means "a woman among us." She asked me to return the favor. I named her Charity and told her it's an old-fashioned word meaning "love."

"And your last name?" she asked, speaking better English than most of the children I'd met.

"Samson."

"Then that is my American name. Charity Samson."

Soon it was time to go. We'd had our pictures snapped, the children gathering around us, the smaller ones settling on our hips, our hands on the soft brown arms that embraced us. I embraced Nothando, tracing a cross of blessing on her forehead, the van becoming my enemy. How could I leave?

I pictured myself in one of those huts. Just a bed, a crate for an oil lamp, books, and simple food from the nearby grocer. I would sit on my stoop and read books to kids. I was old in this vision, with feet widened, flattened from walking around the Swazi roads. At night, I'd bundle myself in blankets since there was no electricity, and I'd sleep inside my walls of mud. I'd learn to stomp on my clothes in a plastic tub, getting hints from the Swazi women on how to get them as clean as they do.

I'd see Nothando each day too. For in that hour, her clinging to my hand, I fell in love.

As we drove off beside the mud houses, I waved through the dirt-caked window. I cried at leaving Nothando behind. Charity. She waved until I disappeared.

It was eight months later that I understood how I could help this girl, this piece of my heart, in Swaziland. I thought that God would immediately tell me what I was to do when I returned to Lexington, but sometimes God takes his time revealing it to us — or we stubbornly believe our way is better. In my case, it was a little of both.

All those months, writing everything down, thinking of not a single way to help Nothando and others like her. Why had I even gone to Africa? Who cares about a typical American woman on a mission trip? Where's the story? But maybe it's to tell you that God can use anybody. I'll tell you how I helped Charity later, though — first we need to continue on the journey through Swaziland.

Supper's ready. Let's sit at the table and talk while we eat.

NOT SO DIFFERENT

Ty

The village of Mangwaneni, where Pastor Sam ministers and Charity lives, is a holler — a hollow if you don't live in Kentucky or West Virginia. In the Kentucky/West Virginia Appalachian region, hollers are everywhere, tiny valleys between mountains where houses are clustered next to each other like acorns on an oak tree. Usually, a holler is full of trash, and Mangwaneni was no different. Let's just say you don't see garbage trucks in Swaziland.

We made our way through this stricken area, stopping every so often to bless children, making an invisible sign of the cross on their forehead like our priest does with ashes or with oil, silently praying that Jesus would come to them — Jesus, the suffering servant who suffers with us. We had no holy oil, just the wish for Jesus to visit them, to comfort them, to give them his hope and his peace.

The sun pummeled us that day like a hot wet blanket as up  the hillsides of the village we hiked. We crested the hill and entered the poorest section of this community. Everyone lived in small, crumbling mud huts, and pungent odors rolled in and out of the twisting alleys. Giant pigs roamed the trash. Then I realized — I was looking at normal, everyday life.

We passed out stickers to the children who surrounded us. Every time they looked at us, the small girls and boys erupted into laughter at the color of our hair. While we couldn't communicate with most of the kids, there was one little girl who stood out. She was a beautiful child who could speak perfect English. She ignored the stickers and began to talk to us.

Nothando (my mom renamed her Charity) told us her dreams — she wanted to be a secretary in a police office. I tried to smile, but inside I couldn't understand, given her intelligence, why her dream seemed so petty. In different circumstances, Charity could've accomplished anything she wanted, but living here in Swaziland she was statistically unlikely to make it even to the age of twenty.

I wanted to sneak her on the plane with me. Knowing she's

stuck over there, in that terrible life, is something that makes the leaves of my faith wilt and tremble. I wonder what she's doing now. I wonder if she's alive. I hope she will defy the statistics, but I picture this girl falling prey to evil men, to a deadly disease, to starvation.

Mangwaneni introduced me to severe poverty; now, after working in Appalachia, I see houses that resemble this community. But at the time I was frozen in shock. These villagers cooked, slept, and raised their children in small mud huts that are falling apart as you read this. They lived — they still live — literally in the midst of a garbage dump.

What can I do? That the question is a cliché doesn't make it pointless to ask. The only time it's a bad question is when it's rhetorical.

When the time came to go, the village kids were so disappointed. Charity made me promise that I would come and visit her again. That is a promise I will try my hardest to keep, but come on — I have a life to live here in America. Going to college, working, dating. What can I do?

That question is why I sleep a lot less now. It's why I want to sleep more.

22

⊘⊘⊘

A WOMAN AND HER LITTLE DOG

We hear the phrase *the other* bandied about these days. Some people use it in a good way, as in "love God and love others." But some view "the other" through a lens of suspicion and superiority. For me, smelly, crazy drunks in Lexington are "the other" in a bad way; the children of Swaziland are "the other" in a good way.

Maybe it's about whom I choose to love.

The only trouble is that the guy who gives me my marching orders says that God loves the world, and I'm pretty sure the world includes every *other* I can imagine.

In Swaziland, each person dying of AIDS is "the other."

After our visit to Mangwaneni, we drove down the highway back toward Manzini, billboards reading, "Stop AIDS — keep the promise!" lining the road. It is unclear what this means in a culture where husbands are under little social compunction to remain monogamous. Dennis said nobody's really figured it out yet. We were on our way to see firsthand what AIDS looks like in one of those back rooms of denial. Ka-Khoza lay before us. Pastor Sam, along with Happiness and their two daughters, led the way in his small car.

We parked in the lot of a general market, locked up the van, and carefully worked our way around the people heading in and out of the store. We were given fair warning before we stepped down onto the snaking, narrow path beside the store that led us into the slum of Ka-Khoza — a collection of slipshod dwellings and shelters and some stick and mud houses littered among beaten footpaths and sheltering trees. According to Dennis, this wasn't a place to go by yourself once darkness settled in.

"It's fine in the day though," he said.

Yeah, thanks for that. However, living downtown, I knew what he meant.

We got our fair share of stares from people coming and going on this path. By this time we were getting used to it. We moved aside to let them pass, men on their way to work or to catch a van into Manzini, women with braids or their heads covered. They seemed different from the Swazis out in the countryside, suspicious, openly challenging us with their gaze.

I didn't blame them. What in the world was a group of foreigners doing in a slum?

The worst heat we'd endured so far beat down like a heat lamp inches from our skin, and I prayed a migraine wouldn't settle in as we followed the beaten path past stick and mud homes in poor condition, past more people treading toward the entry to the settlement, past a roofed steel structure much like the one in the village of Mangwaneni in which Pastor Sam held services on Sunday afternoons. Most pastors have more than one congregation.

We then stepped into the home of Inhlanhla, a church member with HIV/AIDS. The home was in better shape than most, pink paint, peeling but still visible, covering the walls of the main room. There was a table, several chairs set up near the window, and a surprising poster of the Virgin of Guadalupe tacked up in the corner. Sam talked to Inhlanhla, encouraged him, settling his hand on the small man's shoulder, his squeeze compacting the softness of the plaid shirt, his low voice soothing as Inhlanhla bowed his head, hair shorn close, sweat glimmering on his features.

"Inhlanhla's first wife was taken by the virus, and both of his children, ages nine and eleven, have AIDS," Dennis told us as we stood there. "His second wife is with their eleven-year-old son at the hospital. The nine-year-old is staying with her grandmother."

Inhlanhla's back was bowed, exhaustion having become a permanent physical characteristic. He shook our hands and tried to smile.

Inside the main room of his home, he'd stacked the planks he sets up each Sunday for church benches, and in the corner stands the pulpit from which Pastor Sam preaches words of comfort, telling of a Savior who knew pain like we do, who suffered like we do, and who longs for us to be comforted, to give him our heavy burdens.

This sweet, dying man set up church each week for others to worship, others who dwelled in the same slum he did. Sitting in the comfort of my own home, a hand of helplessness wrings my heart. I wonder if Inhlanhla still heads off to work, back bent, knowing that tomorrow will not—cannot—bring healing. I know Pastor Sam is by his side at least. People like Sam and Happiness understand what *other* means in ways I wonder if I'll ever grasp. Esteeming others better than ourselves is difficult in this day of "putting up boundaries."

The farther Pastor Sam led us into Ka-Khoza the more we were looked at askance by those traversing the paths. Pastor Sam needed to check on someone, though, and he led us deeper and deeper into the slum.

Lillian wasn't home. I stared at her small dirt lot fenced by wire attached to sticks in the ground; some tin roofing and plastic formed the perimeter as well. A little gate cut from a piece of corrugated tin about two and a half feet high let us into her yard. More tree limbs had been driven into the ground. A tin roof sat on three walls constructed of rusted slabs of metal and corrugated roofing. The front wall of the makeshift shelter was missing. The floor was dirt. Trash edged the yard, and her only possession, a washing bowl, sat on a stump.

Corn grew outside her compound, green and fresh, and the sun and breeze filtered through the leaves of the trees overhead. It was like a place kids might create in the forest, a place for eight-year-old girls to pretend they were keeping house as they put on fake adult voices, calling everyone "dear" and "darling" while pouring fake tea.

The only difference was that this place was Lillian's real home.

I wondered what it was like when it rained. And when it was cold. Did Lillian huddle on the ground beneath a mound of filthy, moldering blankets? Did she even have any? Dennis told us robbery is epidemic in Swaziland, and blankets are especially precious.

The tin gate opened, and Lillian entered her yard. I laughed at her little fawn-colored dog that had been wagging its tail and begging to be petted during our arrival, only to leap to its feet in a frenzy of outraged yapping as if to strut for its mistress's inspection.

Lillian smiled at us. We pointed at the dog and made the yapping motion with our hands; she said something in siSwati that I figured meant, "His bark is worse than his bite."

Lillian wore a simple cotton dress in shades of red and white, an apron of blue and white, and a head wrap, all worn and soft but clean. Camouflage plastic sandals covered her feet. Her eyes were kind. I shook her hand, pressing my left hand at the elbow of my right arm as I bowed a little. What an honor to touch a hand that had done so much. I understood what such a gesture meant then, showing respect, not strength like we tend to show so often when we shake hands in our own culture, realizing that the person's hand we're shaking has much to teach us.

Lillian guided us to her brother's house just across the path from her home. Pastor Sam invited us to pray for him, so we all filed in. The smell of death had oozed into the very walls. The mud-walled room was so dim that I waited several minutes for my eyes to adjust, but while that sense was catching up, my nose took over, telling my brain a bucket of excrement was hidden somewhere. God truly kept me from gagging.

Phineas lay alone on the bed. A rough blanket covered his torso, while his legs stuck out from beneath the folds. The full heat of the summer day brought out a heavy slick of sweat on my back, but he had pulled the blanket around his chin. The man was skin and bone, the flesh of his face shrunken and exposing his teeth. Eyes listless, yet watching through the watery fog of illness, he reminded me of that poor woman at Manzini Hospital.

I was convinced I needed to see what really goes on in our world, but my certainty crumbled at the foot of Phineas's bed. I felt like a voyeur, observing for my own purposes the suffering of a man made in the image of God.

AIDS was killing Phineas, but Lillian said he was dying of sugar diabetes. It's always something else, right?

Phineas is dead now, I'm sure. Perhaps Lillian is living in his house, not in the "playhouse" across the path.

But that day we prayed for Phineas, Pastor Sam asking for healing. (Did he believe it would happen more than I did? I hope so.) It seemed to give Lillian comfort, and perhaps she was able to pass some of it off to her brother. Who can really know these things? Who can understand?

I left that day feeling that all we do is like a twig trying to hold back Niagara Falls. Why bother? Why not just go home and live the good life, because clearly, my pittance would be like offering one sandwich to a stadium full of people, and my faith was far from able to move a mountain.

DYING ... BUT NOT REALLY

Ty

One of the biggest problems in Swaziland is that no one will admit there's a problem. Perhaps they think that by hiding it, they can convince themselves nothing bad is really happening. Sound familiar?

In Swaziland, people disappear after their AIDS has progressed to a certain point. One day you'll see them, and the next they're gone — put in a back room somewhere to die. Generally, these back rooms are damp, muggy, and dark.

The man we saw in Ka-Khoza lying in his coffin-like bed looked like a living corpse. I'd never before been face-to-face with suffering of this magnitude. We gathered around Phineas and his sister, Lillian, and prayed.

We prayed and prayed and prayed.

Even those of us not speaking aloud prayed in our hearts. We knew, barring a miracle, that this man's life could not be spared, so we prayed for his misery to end. And we prayed for the family he would leave behind — his tiny family that consisted of just his aging sister. She would soon be all alone. Her face revealed her sadness, and her lines seemed to grow deeper before our eyes. Lillian knew her loneliness was about to get far worse, and she could do nothing about it.

On that muggy day, I prayed for Lillian. I prayed that God would send her a companion, someone to take care of her as she had taken care of so many other people in her lifetime. I prayed somebody would answer that call.

I have no idea if somebody has.

23

A MODERN-DAY DEMONIAC

The story of the demoniac in the New Testament has always struck a chord with me. We all have our inner fears. One of mine is that I'll go insane someday. So when I picture a man possessed by demons, living naked around the tombstones and hurting himself, my heart aches with both empathy and fear. When Jesus encountered the man and drove out the demons, a legion of them, he left the man "dressed and in his right mind" (Mark 5:15). I picture myself sitting on a mausoleum, wearing some sort of robe and wondering what to do next—but I've been touched by Jesus, so there is hope.

The next day dawned like the one before it—hot, sunny, and dry, the waves of heat shimmering over the blacktop as Dennis drove us back into Pastor Walter's territory. Back through the rolling hills and then over the dirt roads, we all waved to the schoolchildren by this point and didn't think a thing about the cows walking along the road. We were going to check on Thembela, a woman who fit the role of the demoniac in a way. Although no one told me she was possessed of an evil spirit, she was certainly possessed of a terrible temper.

We pulled up to her property and climbed out, making our way over dirt and stones toward the gate. The hillside of her property gave way to the view of a valley beneath, a swath of green patterned by other homesteads, the blue sky governing the inhabitants. At one time she had a two-room house, but a severe storm had blown away the roof and caused two of the walls to crumble. She was living in a tent provided by the Red

Cross, and at the time of our visit, she was not home. I never met Thembela, but I hope to someday.

Tom related her story. Thembela had a boyfriend. Their relationship was tempestuous, to put it nicely, characterized by loud arguments and fighting that sometimes resorted to slaps and blows. One day, a red rage filling her head, she took a machete to her boyfriend's legs and hacked at them, the blade eating into his flesh, crippling him for life. I don't know about you, but I think someone capable of that kind of violent anger seems far from inheriting the kingdom.

I come from a respectable lot. We're clean and neat, we always wash our hands after using the bathroom, and we try not to admit our shortcomings — because surely our perfection is the greatest testimony to God's work in our lives. What would we do with a woman like Thembela in our ranks? People would think God was ineffective. Besides, let's face it, a woman like her would be high maintenance, and we need help in the children's ministry — a position, I might add, that someone with Thembela's temper would be totally unqualified to fill. We need more people to serve, not *be* served.

Pastor Walter thinks that attitude is useless. We walked around Thembela's property, lingering near the foundation of a new home the church was slowly building for her, bit by bit, as money came in and people's schedules provided the time. We inspected her old home, its pieces lying in ragged bits across the cement floor. The remaining walls leaned in, perhaps remembering the rage of Thembela before she found Jesus. Perhaps she beat at them with her fists too.

She accepted Pastor Walter's invitation to his church, and as her anger began to dissipate, her faith began to grow. A family of three orphans lives down the hill from Thembela now. She keeps an eye on them, and no one thinks that's a bad idea.

Here's what I'm saying: judging simply isn't our job. What we do is love in the name of Jesus, keep showing up, and let God do the rest. Oh, and pray like everything depends on it.

"And they left her sitting there, dressed and in her right mind ..."

Is anything too hard for God?

24

LOLLIPOPS AND GROWING UP TOO SOON

It was by far the warmest day of the trip. We set out to Big Bend, about forty miles southeast of Manzini, near the border of Mozambique, a dusty plain that looked more like how I always pictured Africa—scrub growing out in the bush, dry heat rising in glittering waves off the baked ground. If ever a place could be described as godforsaken, this was it. The sun beats down on that plain with as much tenacity as a tanner hammering a hide. I could hardly imagine what it would be like to make my home in such a flat, dry, scorched wilderness, to see my kids run across the hard stones in bare feet, dragging dust into a house of dirt.

Small stick and mud houses sat far away from each other out on this sun-scorched plain, the road a dusty streak marked by the fading tracks of rarely seen vehicles. Bone-thin children pushed wheelbarrows along the road toward the well; many children congregated at the Big Bend carepoint run by Pastor Timba, a sober man so different from Pastor Sam yet just as dedicated.

Tom drove us to a one-room home the size of a garden shed in which two disabled young people live. The teenaged girl cannot walk. Listless, she sits on a mattress inside all day long, her legs, brown dowels, folded beneath her. Her older brother, severely mentally disabled, sat in the yard on a mat, his smile wide as he swayed, his tongue *zzzz-zzzing* against his bared teeth. Only wearing a shirt, it wasn't just his teeth that were bared—but thankfully, I don't think he cared.

Siyabonga, the girl, is so skinny and malnourished that her head practically lolls on her shoulders. She's alone most days. Her brother, Musa, chronologically a man but mentally a two-year-old, can't walk well, and he sometimes crawls into the yard and sits in the shade of a tree all day. In Swaziland, this situation didn't seem that far from being part of the ordinary. Less than a week into our trip, suffering was beginning to look so normal.

Our little team collected some pens and pencils, and I gave the girl my notebook to use as drawing paper. Tom, Dennis, and Pastor Timba, who shepherds this dry and dusty little flock, replenished her shelves with beans, pap, laundry soap, and other staple items. Though the shelves were full, two questions popped into my mind: Would someone come and steal the food from this defenseless girl? Who would fix the food for them in the first place? Their grandmother had died several months before.

When we climbed into the van, I noticed a long-limbed older boy dressed neatly in old khaki pants and a white shirt and standing at the edge of the yard.

"He takes care of them," Dennis said. "Ever since their grandmother passed away."

"How old is he?"

"Twelve."

Imagine: a twelve-year-old boy caring for two severely disabled people on his own. I'll never forget his silhouette, thin as wire, waving to us as we drove back to the carepoint. I thought about the twelve-year-olds I know, and how utterly incapable they would be in that situation. In many ways, I'm glad for that. This boy should still be a child, not the tender, compassionate man he's become before his thirteenth birthday.

We could learn a lot from him.

Tom and Pastor Timba guided us to the house of an old *gogo* (grandmother), Nomvula. One of the strange things about visiting Swaziland is that you see a lot of older people and many younger people, but due to AIDS, the middle-aged group has been decimated.

On foot, we passed a typical stick and mud structure eroded by time and wind and who knows what else.

"Nomvula had been living there, but we were able to build her a new house," Tom said. The new house, one room, was constructed of cinder block and a tin roof. There Nomvula sat on a mattress, weaving a mat from straw and decorating it with candy wrappers.

When we asked how much she wanted for the mat, she suggested twenty-five Rand—about four dollars. How long it takes to weave one of these mats I can't say. I bought the mat, and a smaller one, for one hundred Rand, the amount suggested by Tom. I felt like a crook. Nomvula said in siSwati she was going to take one of the children she cares for to the clinic.

God, have mercy.

Blessed is Nomvula the mourner. Behind her home are the graves of her husband and three children. She sits in the heat and weaves and cares for her grandchildren and other people's children, doing what few others are willing to do. Seems to me London Ferrell, who buried so many people here in Lexington, would bless Nomvula, and each time she needed him he would show up to bury her dead.

At the carepoint in Big Bend the women gave me a bowl of pap and beans. Let me tell you, those ladies know how to throw down some beans. They were delicious, spiced delicately with, it seemed to me, just salt and pepper, and flavorful. They smiled broadly when I tried to express how much I enjoyed it. I resorted to the international communication for *yummy*—hand over my stomach, a roll of my eyes, and a luxurious "Mmmmm!"

A part of me was comforted to know the food served at the carepoints was tasty. After cutting rot off tomatoes at the homeless shelter, it was good to know that these children could view food not just as sustenance but as something enjoyable. Of course, after eating the same pap and beans for years on end, I might feel differently. Here in the U.S., it can take me an embarrassing amount of time to pick the right brand of peanut butter at Kroger.

After the trip, I'd planned to eat only beans and rice and fresh vegetables for Lent. It doesn't sound like much, but it beats having nothing to eat. Tom Davis told me of a Swazi woman who didn't eat for two months. So that year at Lent, Will prepared me a pot of black beans. I bought some veggies at the grocery store. I made rice for two of three meals a day. Breakfast was problematic. Who wants to start their day with beans and rice? My Lenten fast lasted three days. So much for the same thing every day and being thankful.

The carepoint at Big Bend has a cooking shed and another iron building with just the supports and the roof, yet for some reason, everybody congregated in plastic lawn chairs in a sort of structure made of large branches and a tattered red tarpaulin. Inside this ad hoc tent, the hand of sorrow reached in and squeezed my heart once again. Love trickled forth as I held a little boy on my lap.

Picture Samkela. He was four or five years old when we met. Through the glistening moisture of perspiration and the dust of the landscape, his dark skin was almost blue. His baby teeth gapped in the middle when he smiled, with full lips so perfect any model would have gone under the knife for a pair that looked just liked them. When I sat on an old piece of wood, he sat down and rested his little hand on my arm, his friendly eyes meeting mine. And there he stayed. If I was sitting, Samkela was there. He'd run and play when I visited with other kids or the *gogos* (more nodding and smiling really; Naila trained me well), but he always returned to my side.

When Tom, Dennis, and Pastor Timba went into town to get food for the disabled brother and sister we met earlier and for the sweet Nomvula weaving mats in her little house, they returned with a big bag of lollipops. I'm not talking lollipops like you get at the drive-through window of the bank. I'm talking big, round suckers at least an inch and a half in diameter, sitting like sugary planets on top of their sticks. We handed them out to the kids, some of them just back from school, the girls' dark-blue uniforms soft from the wear of the day. Each child held up his or her hands, ripped off the paper, and popped them into their mouths.

I'm pretty sure Samkela has forgotten about me by now, about the minutes we sat side by side beneath a red tarp, but I'll never forget him. I'll remember the feel of his small, lithe body sitting with me, and how we smiled at one another, holding up our lollipops and hitting them together.

My white hand and his black arm were the most complementary colors I've ever seen. I hugged him, feeling his ribs and shoulder blades, and I wondered how long it had been since he'd had a hug. Maybe an hour; maybe a year. I couldn't have known.

The truth is, Samkela changed me. As did Charity. As will anyone responding to a human touch they may not receive from anyone other than you or those who've said yes to God's call to be merciful as he is merciful. Jacob the cook changed me. So has Naila the refugee. Even Jose Carlos the druggie has made a difference in my life. And the people I've failed with have done just as much to show me how far I have to go—Phil the mentally ill homeless man, Carl the con artist.

Everything changes when issues become people. Life becomes both simpler and more complex. Simpler if we truly believe God loves everyone in the world, and more complex as our world expands exponentially. When issues become people, we accept God's plan that we are now Christ's body—his hands, feet, legs, and arms. His smile. His embrace. We wonder how this God who loves so lavishly is sovereign over a world of such pain. We wonder why our Creator allows us to treat one another so terribly or, just as bad, to ignore the suffering of our fellow humans. I still don't have the answer to those questions. I simply know this: the more the followers of Christ act justly, love mercy, and walk humbly, the better things are for everyone. For *the others*. What if every Christian in the world reached out in love and deed to one sick AIDS patient, one lonely orphan, one poor widow, one hungry family?

Why does that sound impossibly hard to us? What if we did it anyway? Shuck life with God down to the cob, and this is what it looks like:

- Love God and your neighbor as yourself.
- Visit the widows and orphans in their distress.
- Love mercy, act justly, and walk humbly with God.

That sounds like a plan. It sounds like a story big enough to contain each of our stories. It sounds like the life of Christ. So simple. So radical. I believe it with all my heart.

Can you live like that? Will you?

DONE

Ty

Big Bend was brutal.

As much fun as we had at the carepoint, especially once the lollipops were distributed, the image of two young mothers sitting underneath that tarp sometimes still appears when I close my eyes. It was scorching hot, the dust swirling everywhere, and the only shade available was found beneath this gaudy tarp. Tiredness seemed to seep from their pores. These women were done. Done with the heat, the struggle. Done with life. The only thing keeping them alive was their children — and their babies likely weren't long for the world.

In my dreams I see the small, beautiful faces of those babies. They had no idea that life might be better, because what they had was all they had ever known — and it was likely all they would ever know. They would never know what it was like to have a big birthday party or to have grilled hamburgers at the kitchen table with family and friends. These children would probably never get to go on a vacation and jump between hotel beds.

An American church has begun sponsoring this carepoint. The building will be finished, and children will continue to be fed. Are those mothers still sitting there? Are their babies?

25

ASBESTOS AND NO BLACKS ALLOWED

We set out early in the morning for Bulembu, northeast of Manzini and sitting right on the South African border, starting out on the same stretch of highway from Manzini that we always seemed to travel. Dennis, easygoing and with a sense of humor, made it easy for us to joke around, sing whatever songs popped into our head, and share our stories. Dennis, soon to be married to a Swazi woman, told us how they met and courted (Swagheli certainly knew how to play hard to get!) as we journeyed once more into unknown territory. Once we left the highway and started the climb into the mountains, the drive could have crippled a person with back problems. Some people might call what Dennis drove the van over "a road"; I'd call it "a wide path," rutted, rocky, and in need of a giant steamroller. Ty and I, together in the backseat of the blue van, bounced almost to the ceiling of the vehicle. I found myself sitting on my left butt cheek to keep my spine from being jammed repeatedly quite so severely.

It's worth it, I thought, looking forward to viewing the pictures we shot as we climbed in elevation toward the highest point in Swaziland—long, sweeping vistas from our eagle-high stopping points, the valleys of Swaziland spread out like a green cloth, the sky an unending blue you felt you could suck into your mouth and taste.

Finally, after ninety minutes in the van, jangling like coins in a change purse, we climbed a hill, and before us, almost tumbling down the hillsides, lay the vacant buildings of Bulembu.

Once a thriving industrial town, Bulembu housed a busy asbestos mine that closed in 2001, leaving a population of 10,000 with no jobs or resources. Most of the inhabitants were left with nothing.

When we arrived, the place appeared to be almost a ghost town. One small store was clinging for its life to the roadside. Several ministries had moved in — the ABC home for children, a child development center, and a place for sexually abused girls run by religious sisters. Atop the far hill sat the Bulembu Lodge, once a beautiful inn and country club for the executives in the mining company. An eerie feeling hit us all, and if it hadn't been Africa, I wouldn't have been surprised to see a tumbleweed roll on by!

We first made our way past miners' small homes with two rooms, dilapidated and now mostly vacant, windows smashed and paint peeling from the wooden siding. The neighborhood broadcast a grayness that brought with it a sense of loneliness and loss. At the bottom of the valley we approached the children's center, a playground (made possible by a twelve-year-old boy in England who thought the kids should have one), and a white, wooden church. A large group of children were playing, running around, climbing, expending energy anybody over the age of thirty wishes they had.

As we started up the hill, the size of the houses grew from two-room shanties to nice middle-class homes, and farther up, larger homes clung to the hillside, sprawling and exotic — at least to this girl from the Baltimore suburbs — with verandas, lush flora, and an abundance of windows to let in the light. They were once inhabited by the executives of the mining company. Finally we made it to the top of the town and the Bulembu Lodge, where we ate a pleasant lunch of crepes and walked around gardens that were being lovingly restored, with palm trees, flowers I'd never seen, and the standard daisies and rhododendron rooting themselves in beds bordered by stone walls and garden gates.

Two years ago, a group of ministry-minded folks bought the town and are now trying to restore it to a self-sustaining community (*www. bulembu.org*) that tourists will visit. Much of this is still a dream.

After eating in the lodge restaurant, we walked over to the country club facilities. Once the country club is fully restored—with the pool in working order and perhaps even the movie theater (where a tree now grows) showing films once again—this will surely be a vacation spot anyone would want to visit. Hopefully the vacationers will provide the much-needed income for all the ministries in Bulembu, as well as jobs for the inhabitants.

I felt a heavy spirit pressing down on me. Ty did as well, turning to me and shaking her head. "It feels creepy here." Racism—another of the powers and principalities that war against goodness in our world—seemed to cling to the very stucco of the walls and the flagstone pavement. A sign outside the country club chapel bore the words "No Blacks" in siSwati. A new church meets there now, and perhaps they keep the sign as a reminder of what the gospel can become when we walk the labyrinths of our own hearts instead of following the narrow path of Jesus. I'm sure the former churchgoers probably had good excuses for not inviting everybody to the party. Who is my church keeping out? How about yours?

When we don't invite everyone God loves to our parties—and that's everyone, period—we can be sure God's going to leave early. After that, it's just a matter of time until the party ends, and the eerie silence is a crumbling testament to the hopeless barrenness of exclusion.

GRASS BENEATH MY FEET

Ty

The drive to Bulembu is one of my fondest memories. I don't think Mom's old bones were quite as happy! Surely it was far less comfortable than our journey from the United States, but I was, by this time, used to the fact that our plans don't always turn out the way we think they will, and it's better to make the best of it.

When we finally reached Bulembu, we visited the Valley of Hope Community Care Center. This school building was nestled between half a dozen trees, and painted on its side were birds and animals and multicolored flowers. The center exuded cheerfulness. Dennis and the woman who ran the ministry were old friends. As she showed us around and introduced us to the children, a light shone in her eyes. I think it was love for the shape of her life and the children she served, as if she couldn't imagine being anywhere else or doing any other thing. She was living her dream — and it made me long for better dreams.

The center works with some nearby women who make jewelry and purses, helping them sell their products online. Besides bringing money to people in this poor area, this venture brings these women into daily community with each other as they sit for hours a day talking, laughing, and creating. Such a different scenario from the one encountered at Big Bend.

We stayed at the care center for a bit while Mom ate a plate of chicken stew on rice — she always has to try everything — before saying our good-byes to the kids and

the workers. After that, we ate lunch at a lovely little inn.
Before the economy collapsed in Bulembu, a lift would transport
the noncancerous asbestos on a tramline from Bulembu to South
Africa. Because of this, Bulembu was influenced by South
African culture and so developed its own version of apartheid.
Throughout the entire town, we could feel the hatred that once
was there. Though our feet walked over manicured lawns, I knew
the reasons they were there in the first place, and I realized
my own white feet would have been welcomed years before, while
Miss Claudia's black feet would not. It was sobering.

 There was
an old country
club with once
beautiful gardens
and pools, now
deserted. I
could picture
people sunbathing,
drinking umbrella
drinks, and having a wonderful time. White people, of course.
Everywhere we looked there were signs in siSwati that read
"Whites Only." The dining hall, the pool, the theatre — even
the church. Each of these places was now deserted. The once
beautiful, well-kept homes were in shambles, windows broken and
doors missing. The entire town was like the skeleton of a once
healthy body.

When we first arrived, I wondered why we received such
mistrusting looks from the few remaining locals. After touring
the town, I understood. We whites would have been the outsiders,
the privileged enemy. And in a way, I still was.

In America it's possible to insulate ourselves from the crumbling buildings and the worn-out faces of those who have been forgotten, of those who — regardless of their race or ours — we think of as "the other." Well, I can't anymore. Not since moving to Lexington and dealing with Patricia at the CAC or Charles, who comes to our house for a plate of food at midnight. It's strange how things work together, how our move from Maryland, a move I resented with my whole heart, prepared me to walk the paths of Bulembu and to pray to God I would never be numbered among the oppressors.

26

A BOY IN THE DUMP

Angels frequent Bulembu. Robin and Gerald run a ministry named ABC—Abandoned Babies for Christ. I'll admit, that sounded a little strange to me. We like to attach positive people and things to the name of Christ. We'd never say Drug Addicts for Christ or Cancer Victims for Christ—rather, No Longer Addicts for Christ or Cancer Survivors for Christ.

But I have to admit, I like the name. Christ meets us where we are, and even abandoned babies are under his watch and care.

The bustle around ABC almost overwhelmed me. Ty loved it. She can't get enough of little kids. I'll admit I never volunteer for the nursery. I'd rather clean twenty toilets or do ten sinks worth of dishes than take a shift dealing with a roomful of small children—and over thirty children live with Robin and Gerald. That right there qualifies them for sainthood as far as I'm concerned. The children were getting their baths and being helped into their jammies by several local women as we finished up our visit.

How many children have Robin and Gerald saved? They don't seem like the type who keep count. But the kids can count on being loved unconditionally. "We set it up like a family here. We're the mother and father," Robin says. "It's important they know that."

ABC became the first adoption agency in Swaziland. Local police now know where to drop off children they find who have been discarded and left to die. Charlotte, a little girl I held in my lap, was found by the river in a garbage bag. Another baby was buried in a shallow grave, the upturned earth noticed by a neighbor, who dug into the hole and found the child.

It all started with a woman with four things — a car, some bread, a jar of peanut butter, and a loving heart.

In the place where Robin, a South African white, was living at the time, many children in a nearby settlement weren't getting enough food to eat, going to school, or receiving care. "I didn't have much, but I figured I could share a sandwich."

A housewife and stay-at-home mother, Robin prayed "Lord, use me" and meant it. She heard about some hungry kids living up the road in a squatter camp. Many were told "I wish you were dead" by the adults in their lives. Some were simply abandoned. She started by making them peanut butter sandwiches.

Prostitution and drugs were rampant; kids were being stabbed for small bits of change. "No godly ways of living," she said. "I came home after visits and got in the shower, feeling so dirty from walking in this place saturated with evil, with witch doctors."

As Robin showered one day, she envisioned a whirlpool, and the Holy Spirit whispered, "How do you get out of a whirlpool? Someone gets you out. I want you to be that person."

She stood amazed. "How am I going to do this?"

So she fed the children three times a week, way past any reasonable point. Three times a week she took sandwiches to them. For eight years.

Robin was told by the grannies in the settlement about a little boy locked in his shack whenever his mother disappeared. The temperatures exceeded 110 degrees. Robin found the mother and asked if she could take the boy home. William is fifteen now.

Jose came a month later, six weeks old, born to a twelve-year-old mother. Working as a housemaid for a man, this girl became pregnant by him, and he abandoned her. Jose is turning thirteen next month. He arrived with scabies, pneumonia, and severe malnutrition. "We cursed the scabies in Jesus' name, and that's how we got rid of them," Robin said as we sat in the living room drinking tea Gerald made for all of us. I've never cursed a disease, but I believed her! Why wouldn't God respond to one who was so obviously involved in work so dear to his heart?

It wasn't easy.

"For six years we did not preach to the people. They cursed us. One granny, caring for nine children, sent her twelve-year-old granddaughter over the hill to get pap from a man who would rape her. She cursed us too."

Robin was handing out clothes, and an old woman cursed her because of a hole under the arm of one of the garments. Robin decided not to go back — but God showed her Romans 10:14:

> How, then, can they call on the one they have not believed in? And how can they believe in the one of whom they have not heard? And how can they hear without someone preaching to them?

Robin and her workers decided to bless the grandmother instead. They took a packet of clothes and food out to the settlement. "We are sorry for the way we treated you," they told her.

The old grandmother took one look at Robin and burst out crying. She said, "I have never seen love like this before."

"And she was on our side from then on," Robin said.

Robin and Gerald live the lesson that love is never the wrong choice. Love, as Paul wrote to the Corinthians, never fails. And Robin practically paraphrased the thirteenth chapter of that epistle wherein Paul says that even speaking with tongues of angels pales compared to love. "It's not about telling them about Jesus; it's about showing them Jesus."

Robin should know.

Taking tea with us that day was Andrew. This engaging, handsome young man was adopted by Robin and Gerald, and looking at him, I fully believed Andrew may grow up to change his nation for the better. I looked at each child and wondered if this one would be the one — the one to cure AIDS, to bring social change, to create employment, to fight for the rights of women, to return dignity and honor to young Swazi men. With Andrew, it didn't seem like an impossible dream.

Andrew told us his story as we sat in the living room of the ministry house at ABC, still sipping our tea, listening to story after story. The peace inside the house rested upon us. The children didn't yell or wail. Outside, the sun shone on a town once torn by lines of racial oppression; inside, white and black came together, blurring lines of what it means to be a family. Andrew was the son of Gerald and Robin every bit as much as if he'd come from their bodies.

He spoke openly and without much emotion. "My mother had a fight with my father and left when I was little. I never got to meet her; then she died. Father died—I'm not sure how old I was—he had lots of girl-friends. He drank a lot so I wasn't raised up properly. My father left me with his brother, and so I stayed with my uncle and slept under his bed or outside. He abused me, hitting me and all. I hated it and ran away and lived in the streets."

Andrew had no food, and he wore his clothes for months at a time. "If I got anything, my uncle took it."

When Andrew was three, Robin started coming to the squatter camp. "She worked with me and fed me, and she'd tell us about God. I picked up some things from her, and I thought it was good—I didn't know the Lord or Jesus—but I knew whatever I did, I wanted to do good things."

Robin saw Andrew suffering on the street, how he and many of the other children had to eat out of garbage cans. To sleep when he was in the bush, he'd find a plastic sugar bag, crawl inside, gather the top of the bag and pull it in. In winter he'd find a house being built or an old car. Water taps around the area provided a place to drink. "But sometimes I would go for days without food. We called the dump Mother Care because we could find food there."

Mother Care. The dump was Andrew's mother. As a mother, sitting in that room with my oldest child, I recoiled at the very idea of human be-ings, precious children of God, calling a dump their mother. "God, have mercy," I pray even now.

Gerald continued the story. "Robin said, 'How long can he, this older boy, resist smoking, drinking, glue sniffing, and giving in to petty crime?'"

When Andrew came into their home, Robin and Gerald were home-schooling all of their children. He said to Robin, "Please, I want to read."

"Why?" Robin asked.

"Because I want to read the Bible."

Gerald nodded. "His wanting to read God's words has opened up his mind. In three years he's gone from grade 1–2 to grade 7. The Lord has opened up his mind."

Gerald, who grew up believing not only that racism was acceptable but that black Africans were a subspecies, has been disinherited by his family in Mozambique because of his love for his black children. The affection between Gerald and Andrew is so palpable I could taste it like honey on a biscuit.

Robin brought Andrew to live with them when he was eleven.

"I see how I could have died, how I was chased by dogs, dangerous things in the squatter camp. Everyone does what they want, and I felt left out because I didn't do what they wanted to do. But when I tried, I couldn't do it. After I was with a family who cared for me and loved me, I knew that Jesus loved and cared for me, and I decided to welcome him into my life."

We serve a God of reconciliation. In a town built on racism, Andrew, Gerald, and Robin are living proof.

ROLE MODELS

Ty

After adopting Andrew, Gerald and Robin became more aware of the abandoned children in Swaziland. This is when they decided to start the home for abandoned children. In their home, there are babies everywhere. Little African babies who have been given British-sounding names such as Charlotte, George, Colin, and Christopher, as well as Swazi names. And all of these beautiful children were, at one time, abandoned. All of the children there would not be with us if it weren't for Gerald and Robin.

Some of the kids are HIV positive, but they are all given their ARVs and receive close medical attention. Robin and Gerald want to make sure these children have the best life possible, so they carefully attend to their special needs, hurting when they hurt, praying for them, and always giving them hope.

They view all of these kids the same way they view their own children, speaking of their accomplishments with pride, laughing with them, weeping when some of them have to leave and go back to what for some of them are terrible home situations. They acted so naturally, scooping them up, setting them down, running their hands atop little heads. And without an ounce of pride, self-congratulation, or self-righteousness. I viewed a living portrait of how to love others, and I wanted in.

How that will work itself out remains to be seen. But I've seen firsthand the grace of God in miraculous ways. I've watched him love the forsaken through people who simply made themselves available, people who bear all things, believe all things, hope all things, endure all things.

Can I ever be like them?

27

⟡⟡⟡

WOLVES WITH PITIFUL FACES

I'd like to say that all the nonprofit organizations at work in Swaziland are godly. I'd like to report that most of the money we give makes it to the people we're trying to help, so that as many lives as possible are saved. It would be great. And there *are* great organizations out there — Children's HopeChest for example — which is why I felt comfortable traveling with them and writing this book.

One evening during a meal at our hotel, we were talking with Jumbo, the faithful servant who ministers mercy and compassion in Swaziland and picks up weary travelers like us from the airport. Jumbo is from South Africa, a white man who's given his life to the Swazi people. He's a giant and quite the imposing character.

Jumbo told us about some shady characters in the world of international aid. Most of us can't fathom people who will exploit the poor and the suffering to fill their own pockets, but such people do exist. It wouldn't be so bad if they were only taking pictures, and not harming anyone. But some organizations have actively preyed on the minds and the purses of those who have almost nothing to give.

"They are wolves in sheep's clothing," Jumbo told us.

One organization, a very large, popular sponsorship program, would sometimes arrange for photo ops, bringing sacks of food, handing out T-shirts emblazoned with their logo, distributing food for the benefit of the cameras and the donors who were present. Then, once the cameras and the higher-ups were retreating down the dusty road, the remaining food—even as folks stood in line for something to eat—would be loaded back onto the truck. And off they'd go. This major charity, which Christian ministries tout and music artists support at their concerts (some of them actually receive a per-child fee for the scholarships they garner), was kicked out of Swaziland. Since then, they've been allowed back in, and the new director is cleaning house. Thank God.

Something similar happened to Pastor Walter with another organization that brought in food, first aid kits, and signage—everything to make the Agape carepoint look like their own operation. A week before a media event, they told Pastor Walter to have windows installed in the main building and a toilet built.

Yeah right. With what money?

Naturally, Pastor Walter refused, so the organization borrowed windows from neighbors' houses and erected a toilet building in a week. Signs went up in the new school building and all around the carepoint. They had people give fake testimonies and handed the *gogos* speeches to say for the cameras and put them in those blasted T-shirts.

The photo op went as planned, the bigwigs arriving and most likely thinking what a great job their group was doing for the people of Swaziland. Into the cars they climbed, blind to the truth. After all was said and done, the local organizers pulled out the windows and took down the signs—even the alphabet strips in the school building weren't safe. The *gogos*, asking if they might be paid a little for what they had done, were reprimanded for inquiring.

Then the organization loaded it all up and drove away.

Ever imagine God throwing up?

"At least we ended up with a new toilet," Pastor Walter said with a shrug.

Thank goodness this particular organization was secular and wasn't doing anything in the name of God or because of their supposed love for Christ.

Jumbo's words are haunting. "People appreciate everything you do for them, but they are damaged by broken promises."

With all the broken promises, all the many wounds to heal—wounds often inflicted in the name of the God who is love—one must even be careful where to take a picture. Swazi people are tired of folks coming in, snapping their image, and using it for publicity for an organization that never helps. They're tired of being used.

On the way back to town after visiting Big Bend, we stopped the car so I could take a picture of the sunset. The sunsets in Swaziland are clearly outlined, the oranges, pinks, and brilliant purples in sharp focus, settling behind the silhouetted mountains as the earth rolls over against the rays of the sun. As I snapped a photo, a man standing in front of a shanty on the other side of the road reprimanded me. My camera was pointed in their direction. "Why are you taking pictures of us?" he yelled in English.

"The sunset!" I pointed to the sky.

He waved his hand in disgust and turned away as I got in the car. Clearly, he was suspicious and had every right to be.

We so long to give. To sponsor a child, to send a bit of our paycheck every week to a ministry we believe will use most of it to send aid and comfort.

However, it's important to be honest and wise about this. Not every organization out there will give you the best value for your giving dollar. So find out everything you can before you make a donation or sign on to sponsor a child. What percentage of your gift actually gets to the people you're seeking to help?

Like life in general, a good way to give is through relationships. Do you know someone who works for a relief ministry? Can you support a friend or family member who has given time and talent to helping others?

At the very least, when you find an organization, poke around the Internet (not just on the organization's website) and see what others have to say.

There's so little time, and it seems we have few resources to give away—so make sure they count. That part of it is up to you. I'd rather see my money buy beans and rice and shoes and medicine than a fleet of shiny new trucks.

28

⌀⌀⌀⌀

AN EASIER JOURNEY?

The morning awakening in Swaziland felt much like the other days. I'd slept poorly, however, my head spinning with thoughts of all I'd seen and how that would translate into my own culture. It was also the last time we would awaken in this tiny kingdom.

Ty and I packed our duffel and arranged our carry-ons — the computer, the camera bags, books, and toiletries. First off, we were going around to the various markets to buy souvenirs.

The group collected in front of the hotel, our bags sitting beside us or piled on the sidewalk. We didn't have a lot to say as we sat on the stone wall of the garden and the steps leading into the hotel. What was left? Already all we'd seen, heard, and experienced was brewing inside, turning into something that would change the way we viewed our lives, each other, and the world around us.

The vans arrived, and we piled in, heading out to the Swazi Candle Factory, where brightly colored wax had been poured into shapes of seemingly every animal, vegetable, and mineral.

Next we drove to a large market on the outskirts of town, the makeshift buildings in a centipedal line, its segments under low roofs, with only back walls. We entered the dark shops, each one breathing into the next, confronted by wooden objects, textiles, jewelry, and key chains. I chose a wooden meat platter for Will, a length of cloth, and a carved nativity set for our home. I was told to bargain, but I didn't have it in me.

By this time, I knew where those vendors lived; I'd seen what they were facing when they closed up their stalls and went home for the night. How could I take away even a penny from them?

Finally, after a stop at yet another market, this one in the center of Manzini, we left Swaziland, the green mountains pulsing as they ebbed and flowed outside the speeding vans, staying put where we could not. It was time to leave, and our brains were filled with wonder, sadness, and even fear. The problems were so great, the people in such need. *Dear God, what in heaven's name could we do?*

The plane ride home felt anticlimactic. We traveled across the continent of Africa, and after eighteen hours, we deplaned, on time, in Louisville, Kentucky. Will, Jake, and Gwynnie met us in the airport. We received hugs, kisses, and the love of our family. They were all well. We were well.

How could I share that with Swaziland? How could I infuse even one-tenth of the love I felt in that moment?

I did not know.

Back in Lexington

29

MORE LESSONS TO LEARN

After I returned from Africa, I sank into a dark depression. Under the delusion that I would go over there and think of something amazing that would affect thousands of people, I came back feeling utterly helpless. Who was I to believe I could do anything? I was just a writer living in Lexington. I had children to raise, books to write, meals to prepare, bathrooms to clean. I stopped volunteering, my life turning inward, each day a struggle just to get out of bed and go to Mass.

Besides, God, if you want me to do anything, you can tell me. I'm listening. I don't know what you'll come up with, but I can't imagine it'll be anything really helpful in the long run. People are dropping like flies, young girls are being raped. Come on! You've got a big job there. And let's face it, there are people far more dynamic, capable, organized, and prepared for the job—people like Tom Davis, Dennis, Jumbo.

All I could do was pray, and that felt like an excuse.

Where was my faith? Had I gone all the way to Africa only to come back with a terminal case of blaming God?

Honestly, I didn't believe God cared. How could he? I mean, I didn't believe he actually cared about me, Lisa Marie. God the Father only loved me because he loves everyone. I was loved in the lump of humanity. But truthfully, how could a holy God love this failure? Boo-hoo.

What was happening to me?

Knowing I couldn't move Denise the prophetess down to Kentucky with me, God sent me another prophet. Jarrod used to be a Methodist minister and is now a chaplain for people in hospice. Hailing from eastern Kentucky, smack-dab in the middle of coal country, Jarrod has that flair a mountain storyteller possesses, and he brings true cheer to those who are dying.

Despite all of Denise's prophetic words to me—"God knows you love him, but he wants your heart"—I still kept God the Father at arm's length. I understood what he wanted of me, but how to *do* that remained a mystery, and I was in no spiritual shape to begin trying. Enter Jarrod, who, during a time of prayer, zeroed in on my Father issues without me uttering a word. Even an atheist might be tempted to believe something supernatural was afoot.

Just before Lent, at the end of February, Jarrod stopped by, as he does sometimes, to see how I was doing. We sat on my living room couch, the sun streaming in through the picture window behind us, and we prayed together. He asked me, "Do you want to love God the Father?"

I had to think for a minute. I wanted to answer honestly, not just give the answer I was supposed to say if I was a good Christian lady.

"I want to want to." That was all I had.

He nodded. "That's good. That sounds honest. He says there's nothing to be afraid of. He's not going to hurt you."

I wanted to believe that. I really did. But how could I trust him after all I'd seen? And after all I'd been through, having buried both parents and miscarried in a public restroom?

We prayed together, Jarrod's words speaking comfort as the Spirit came into the room and settled in with us. After the "amen" Jarrod gave me some suggestions. I began to read Brennan Manning's books, and at night I'd tell the Father over and over, "*Abba*, I belong to you. *Abba*, I belong to you." To be honest, I felt a little silly, but it's amazing what spiritual desperation will allow you to consider.

Slowly, ever so slowly, something began. It was gentle and almost untraceable, like the settling of a feather on the ground. I found my heart beginning to soften. Just a little. Loving the Father didn't seem like something so darned impossible.

Maybe it was all really true. Maybe that verse that reads "How great is the love the Father has lavished on us, that we should be called children of God!" (1 John 3:1) wasn't put in there just to take up space. Could God really be my Father? Why should he care so much? Why, when he has such bigger things to worry about, like the HIV/AIDS crisis in Swaziland, does he want me plugged into his life so badly?

Jarrod called me just after Lent began. Three days earlier, I'd had ashes crossed onto my forehead and been told to "turn from sin and be faithful to the call of the gospel."

"Just sit back and watch," Jarrod said. "The Father is going to show you how much he loves you. Jesus says don't worry about him; he's glad to step out of the way. He'll be fine."

I've always been a little in love with Jesus. I didn't want to hurt his heart by focusing on the Father. I know this is contrary to everything he said in Scripture about his love for the Father; how if we've seen him, we've seen the Father; how he glorifies in the Father. I'm just a one-man woman I guess. Not an easy place to be when trying to know and love a triune God!

So I continued to pray, laying my head on the pillow each night, praying the Divine Mercy chaplet on my rosary for Samkela and Charity, seeking the possibilities of how I could help the victims in Swaziland. And I continued to inch closer to the Father in heaven, who knew how much I needed to love him, who knew my heart was dying inside, withering without the nourishing light of the Sustainer of the Universe.

Until I could realize that God the Father truly loved me, my spiritual life was malnourished. I didn't really trust God's words to me, and so I missed his daily bread.

I went to work on another novel, went to daily Mass, and received the nourishment of the Eucharist, the daily lectionary readings, and the fellowship of the parishioners at Holy Spirit parish.

Jarrod's words began to bear fruit as God lavished love on me.

That Lenten season was one great happening after another. My book *Quaker Summer* was unexpectedly given two prestigious awards. Will was hired as a professor at a wonderful college nearby. Book sales were growing. I was floored—and thankful. What Jarrod had assured me of was coming to pass. And still, all I could do was pray for Swaziland.

Finally, just shy of Easter, the Father put the cherry on top of the entire confection of affection he'd given me. The women of *communality* were enjoying a weekend retreat at the Sisters of Loretto's motherhouse near Bardstown, Kentucky. A peaceful air surrounded the compound as we drove up the long lane to the grounds. Though it was dark, the lights of the motherhouse, where many religious sisters who had spent their entire lives serving Jesus had come in their old age to retire and live in community together, shone into the mist that was falling. We let ourselves in, unpacked, and settled into the retreat house.

We enjoyed a concert at the chapel and then talked with an eccentric religious sister who was the artist in residence for the order, whose massive sculptures contrasted her tiny stature—and, of course, we ate together and talked with each other, just enjoying the time together. We talked about our personal struggles, sharing our frustrations in raising families alternatively in a culture that honors power and wealth above all else. Just look at who our celebrities are. But the struggle for me was also interior. There were (and are) times I resented my husband for upending our lives, and even then, I was still fighting against that. Yet something appealed to me in the tiny room in which I stayed—just a twin bed and a desk, a crucifix on the wall.

Let me confess something: I fight against materialism. When I first married Will, I was upset because we didn't have a house that first year. (Was I clueless or what?) I pictured myself moving up in the world, belonging to a country club someday, wearing designer clothing, and having the perfect dishware and fine furniture. And shoes? I'd have a closetful someday! I've taken way too many shopping trips, buying things because I liked them, not because I needed them. Our house and cars were expensive.

Despite what seemed like a materialistic lifestyle during our fattest years, there was one item I never allowed myself to buy. Every time a catalog from The Company Store arrived, I would leisurely flip through the pages, enjoying all the colors and textures, because, let's face it, bedding is utterly fabulous. Every time, I'd feel a little longing because I knew "the page" was coming, the one I'd been looking at since I was a young married woman but had never gone so far as to indulge myself and purchase the displayed item.

The luscious down comforter.

Years earlier, I'd purchased a synthetic, down-style comforter on sale, but it couldn't compare to the buttery, puffy yumminess of a real down comforter. I'd spent loads of money on stupid stuff over the years but never dove into the world of down. To this day, I wonder why I didn't. I was able to justify just about everything else I bought but didn't need.

The second evening of our women's retreat at Loretto, we were sitting around the kitchen table with cups of tea and Heidi's amazing chocolate chip cookies sitting in a Tupperware tub in the middle. I'm not sure how the topic came up; I was probably complaining about the cold in my house — we keep it at 60 degrees in the winter — and telling how I throw a quilt in the dryer for five minutes, snatch it out, and run through the house with a "Nobody get in my way!" as I head for my bed.

The women laughed at my antics. My loathing of winter and the chilly house is well known to them after season upon season of complaints. Sherry said, "Don't you have a down comforter? Those heat up right away."

"No," I said. "I've always wanted one. I hear they're great." I wasn't going to tell her about all those wistful glances at the glossy catalog pages over the years.

"My mother bought us an extra one. You're more than welcome to have it if you'd like."

Only God knew of that desire. Only he knew the one thing he could give me that would say, "It's all true. I love you. I know you. Everything about you. I want you to have the one desire of your heart you never allowed yourself."

And so, at forty-three years of age, I finally, truly, gave my heart to God my Father. It wasn't a flash of realization or a momentous epiphany. The love of God collected in the thirsty recesses of my heart, drop by drop, until the parched ground grew fertile. It was more than belief that

Jesus died for me; my faith became something childlike and filled with wonder. I trusted! Finally! I trusted that he loved me. I could love him back, and it would be OK. No matter what storm came my way, what pain and disappointment lay ahead, he would be surrounding me. He would be my friend. He would love me through this life, whatever came my way.

◈◈◈◈

What does this have to do with justice?

God's great love for me means I can't misrepresent that love to anyone else. His great love is the model for how to run our charities and churches. Above all, his love shows us how to love each other.

Love at the heart of justice? Saint Paul wasn't merely babbling when he wrote, "If I give all I possess to the poor ..., but have not love, I gain nothing" (1 Corinthians 13:3).

Service without love is the surefire recipe for burnout. Know you're loved by God the Father; draw close to him. You can trust him. If *you* can, so can the world. But it's up to us to show them.

JUST BECAUSE

Ty

Africa solidified the calling I received when my godmother washed my feet and told me I was destined to work with the poor, to love those no one else would. Sometimes I imagine what that will look like; other times I experience it firsthand. This year, during a gap year between high school and college, I've been privileged to work with children in the foothills of Appalachia. The poverty and pain right here in my own state mirrors what I saw in Swaziland — children abandoned by their parents to be raised by a family member, drug addiction, illness, lack of work, lack of hope. I've held children who have addicted mothers, bandaged the wounds of a girl beaten up by her boyfriend, and driven pregnant teenagers to the county clinic.

I've also laughed a lot with my boss, Lisa, and her family, sitting around her father's table with a Stouffer's lasagna and some garlic bread, listening to their stories. What strikes me the most about these people, as well as Dennis and Jumbo, is that mercy and justice, compassion and love, are just something you do if you love God. They don't make a big deal about standing up for justice or make an angry hue and cry over injustice. They live the life. They do good because, well, why wouldn't you? People need help. Who turns their back on that?

I'm reminded of what a lot of people say when a reporter interviews them after they've done something heroic — jumping into an icy river to save a drowning child or running into a burning building to bring out a child crying in her crib. "I just did what anyone would do," they say, almost without fail.

Really?

I'm not so sure anyone would. But I want that to be my response now. Not to go in as the savior, the do-gooder, the person who believes she will be the one to turn it all around. I just want to be a good person, to do what I do because it's simply what you do when someone needs you.

My mom asked me how my experience in Swaziland changed me. And the answer is, "Not as much as I'd hoped for." I wonder if it really changed anybody. We seem to be going about our lives in much the same way, only we know more now about the suffering in our world. Some of us have chosen to alleviate it as best we can; others of us simply feel more sadness than we did before—but life carries its own responsibilities.

Can a single trip do that much for anyone? Maybe it's a stepping-stone across a stream. And each forward motion leads us to look more like Jesus, act more like him, and care for others the way he did. That's my prayer these days—a step forward here, another there, and maybe then, little by little, we can make some small difference.

Each day we try here in Lexington. It might be helping Crystal to read at the after-school program or giving an addict a plate of dinner on our porch, or it might be praying for Charity in Swaziland as she grows up.

Maybe Swaziland taught me this more than anything: something is better than nothing, and all those somethings add up to something more. We may never even know what it is.

Maybe someday we can all say, "I just did what anyone would do," because it would be the norm, not the exception to the rule. I pray this for everyone who loves God, I pray this for my family, I pray this for myself.

In the end, however, we're all in God's hands.

Perhaps that's what I learned more than anything else.

30

MATTHEW'S VISION OF JESUS

The entire journey to Lexington, to Africa as well, began in my heart years ago when I was a teenager. It's easy to say God suddenly rained down the truth on me that I needed to reach out to those who need the love of God in tangible ways. But I have to be honest. I always knew, deep down, that being a Christian meant more than taking care of me and mine.

I was fifteen when I bought my first Keith Green album. I remember getting my mother to drive me to Baptist Book Store in Lutherville, Maryland. Contemporary Christian music was new to me, and I thought, "Wow! Sign me up for this stuff!"

As it is with prophets, Keith Green hit me right between the eyes. But in particular, his musical retelling of Matthew 25, Jesus' story of the sheep and goats, planted a seed that lay dormant for years. But I felt it there, like a hard kernel in the soft flesh of my heart.

Perhaps the realization of what following Jesus meant wasn't so much a new thing but the watering of something much older waiting to be awakened.

We can find many places in which to be the living words of Jesus in Matthew 25. Do people hunger? Feed them. Thirsty? Give them a drink. Sick? Care for them. In prison? Go to them. Lonely? Knock at their door.

I still read this passage occasionally, trying to ingest the words, to water that message of Jesus so that it grows into something full and beautiful. But if you read the book of Matthew, before you ever get to the sheep and the goats you have to make your way through the Beatitudes in chapter 5.

As I read them now, however, something different happens. People come to my mind, those who inhabit the Word of Christ. I remember Swaziland and my neighbors and friends in Lexington.

When Jesus says, *"Blessed are the poor in spirit,* for theirs is the kingdom of heaven,"* I think, Blessed are you, faithful *gogos,* who walk to your carepoint to cook for the orphans. You have your own troubles surely, but you still show up and care for those who have even less than you. Bless you.

And those who mourn? Blessed are you. Nomvula, may God bless you. You have three children and a husband buried in your back yard, and still you sit on your mat and weave. More children live with you now. They came; you cared. Bless you, dear sister. Bless you, Priscilla the refugee, who left the dead behind you, who mourn their presence as you make your life with us.

And the meek. Young man at Big Bend, you care in complete obscurity for the mentally and physically disabled. You are too young for such responsibility, and nobody asked you to do this. But still you show up each day to make sure they are all right. Bless you, little brother. Naila, you bake bread, though your own life is filled with uphill climbs and you cannot speak our language.

Oh, *those who hunger and thirst for righteousness,* be filled. Andrew, you were living in a garbage dump—Mother Care—and many around you were succumbing to a life you didn't want. And who could blame them? But you wanted more. You wanted to be righteous. And God gave you a family. Bless you. Jacob, I don't know where you are. Perhaps you're strung out on cocaine somewhere nearby. But I pray that someone will help you find the way home.

And *my friends who are merciful,* may much mercy be shown to you. Jumbo and Kriek, Robin and Gerald, Dennis and Tom, all who labor for the people of Swaziland, people who have the gifts and talents to work for themselves and live the high life but don't. Bless you, dear sister and brothers. Sherry, Will, and Ty, bless your efforts here in Lexington.

The pure in heart will see God, Nothando. Charity. You took my hand and led me through your village, and you loved me right away. Bless you, little sister. Samkela, you sat on my lap and smiled while we ate lollipops. I didn't want to leave you there alone. Either of you. Bless you, children.

Pastors Walter and Sam, *blessed are you as you make peace* when you share the gospel and bring food, clothing, and education to your people. You are truly sons of God. Bless you, my brothers.

As we sit here in my living room, looking around at my possessions, many of them reminders of my old life, I want you to look away and look at the people you have met on our journey together and at God's definition of being blessed, and know that I pray this for you now: May you, like those above, be blessed to be a blessing, to love with a full heart and open hands, to visit the widows and the orphans in their distress, to give comfort to the dying, healing to the sick, and sight to the blind.

Jesus, show us the way.

POSTLUDE: COMING HOME

So what became of our trip? What did God tell me to do? Did I ever get my act together? Well, in the words of Willy Wonka, "We have to go backward to go forward."

But what could we do now? Here?

We could sew! There were children in rags! This was more than just throwing money at the problem. I knew a lot of women who would gladly spend an hour a day at their machines making simple skirts and shorts for little boys and girls who'd most likely never had a new garment of their own.

After I got home, I purchased a sewing machine, some fabric, and a pattern book and set about to make the prototype for a simple skirt. I enlisted several other women, organized them into an email group, and found places online where I could buy discounted fabric, keeping the garments to a dollar apiece, and polo shirts we could buy in bulk for two dollars. This was going to be great—all over Swaziland, little boys and girls would proudly pull on their first new outfit!

First, though, we were going to outfit Pastor Sam's schools with uniforms. We'd stood by the building, and he talked about how nice it would be if his kids had uniforms like the schoolchildren who could afford the government schools.

The kids in the village of Mangwaneni and nearby would be able to go to Sam's school with their heads held high! We were going to do this thing. It was achievable. It was going to happen.

It didn't happen.

It's usually a good idea to get to understand a culture a little better before you offer to help. After proposing the idea, the folks on the ground in Swaziland didn't think it was a good idea. The uniforms coming in from an outside source would not have been the proper way to go about it. After all, Swazi people could be put to work making them. We needed to bring employment too.

To be honest, being rebuffed like that made me mad. I had people here willing to help. They wanted to really "do" something. And one lady, a dear friend, is in tight financial straits. She has plenty of *time* to give, but I couldn't ask her for a check. I sat and stewed.

And stewed.

Who were they to tell me I couldn't sew outfits? I mean, really! Couldn't I just sew anyway?

For seven months I sat and stewed. I prayed for Charity, and I thought about that iron structure on the hill of Mangwaneni. The only thing I could do to further that was to raise money.

Really? Raise money? Had I gone all the way to Africa for that?

Pastor Sam could have that school completely outfitted and ready to go with just a little money sent his way—little by American standards. But I didn't want to be a fund-raiser. This was the woman who'd rather spend hours and hours writing this darned book than ask for money, remember?

OK, Lord. You want me to try and make things better in that village? Fine!

But the fact was, I knew Pastor Sam now. I knew his wife, Happiness. I knew Charity. And I loved them. I wasn't just throwing a check at some faceless problem. I knew what the need was, and I needed to respond. Maybe that was the difference.

I headed across the street to my friend Billy Ray's porch. Billy Ray knows his way around the event-planning biz, and maybe he could tell me how to throw a fund-raiser. It was a little bit like asking a doctor to look at the weird spot on your underarm. He wasn't a bit helpful with the information I sought. I think he might have thought I was hitting him up. So we sat and talked about something else and watched the cars go by. He did offer me this bit of advice: "Just make up a nice letter about it and send it to everybody you know first. You might be surprised."

Yeah, thanks for that. That's asking people for money, remember?

I grumbled my way back home across the street.

But then I thought about it. What could it hurt? Honestly? I'd just send it to people I knew would love me anyway. I'd give them plenty of opportunity not to respond, lots of outs. I wasn't asking them to support *me*, after all. I wasn't asking them to take out a second mortgage or anything. And any little bit would help.

OK, Lord, I grumbled, *Here I go, commencing the most humiliating act of my life. Asking for money.*

I pulled up a blank page and began.

I wrote about Charity. Pastor Sam. The woman who cared for five children, who allowed her food to burn while she showed us hospitality. I wrote about the school. About how, after a private donation of $12,000, we needed roughly $13,000 to finish everything, from walls, to electrical, to a well, to tables, chairs, and chalkboards.

I added pictures of the village children. I used orange for the headings. I tried to jazz it up without making it too professional and slick looking — believe me, that wasn't hard! And then I hit Send with a massive knot of fear in my stomach. What if everybody got mad at me? I *did* put the "prayer escape clause" in there: *If you can't give, your prayers would be so helpful.* And I even meant it!

And so I waited, checking my email every minute and a half, wondering if I was going to get reamed out by someone.

Thanks be to God, my fears were unfounded. Replies began to flow in. Folks were so supportive and kind. And they were ready to help. Billy Ray was right.

As of this writing, my friends have helped raise all the funds to build the school, and I've seen pictures of the nearly completed building. There in Swaziland, a village will have fresh water from a new well, a better kitchen for their carepoint, and their own school building. Pastor Sam will have his own church building. What I'd learned in Lexington, that community matters, came back in abundance as people I loved rallied together.

I'm going back there soon. Maybe they'll let me teach a class or stay for a while. Maybe what was started on that hour-long visit last year will blossom into something long-term. It's my prayer.

This book is about more than Swaziland. It's about more than God replacing a suburban family's American dream with dreams of the kingdom. It's about the God who gives us the courage to do what we never thought we could. It's about Robin with her sandwiches, saving babies in garbage bags, and Claudia and Andrea feeding a dying woman in the hospital. It's about Dennis, Jumbo, and Kriek serving day after day, hour upon hour, and still finding strength. Tom running all over the world on behalf of orphans. Pastors growing corn and burying the dead. It's about Sherry helping refugees and Ty working with underprivileged children. It's about what goes on each day at the Catholic Action Center and the home for unwed mothers.

It's about you, me, all of us, loving God and loving our neighbors as ourselves.

Who is my neighbor?

I'll let you be the judge of that.

God gives food to the hungry and strength to the weary, sight to the blind and hearing to those who are deaf. What is it, O man, that God requires of you? "To act justly and to love mercy and to walk humbly with your God" (Micah 6:8).

I'm sorry it's taken so long for me to tell you my story—I see your after-dinner tea is cold, and your legs are probably falling asleep on our rickety couch! Can you come back tomorrow? We'd love to hear your story too. Take as long as you want. What brought you here, and where do you think God might be calling you?

APPENDIX: SOCIAL JUSTICE IN SCRIPTURE

@@@@

On this journey, I've had a few people think I stopped being faithful to the Bible with all my talk of social justice. (God is a conservative Republican to some people, believe it or not.) Will and I have always been a little mystified by this, as we never heard a sermon on the poor in all of our years growing up. No wonder folks of that same ilk felt we were turning our backs on Scripture — they probably hadn't heard such sermons either. And there aren't a host of books lining the shelves of Christian bookstores with titles such as *5 Steps to Selling All You Have* or *God, Defender of the Helpless: Book One in the Character of God Series*. But the fact is, Scripture is filled with talk about the poor, and to be faithful to the Word of God means paying attention to a topic that gets so much airtime.

So, if you're like me, and you'd like more of a reason than my words to encourage you to serve others, make your way through the following list of social justice Scripture texts from the New International Version of the Bible. The list is by no means exhaustive, but even these few pages will help you see how important our involvement is to God, how precious his poor are to him. It was compiled by Rick Webster, teaching pastor at The Third Space in Peterborough, Ontario (see *www.thethirdspace.net*). I found his categories most helpful. And as you read, pray over each verse, asking God to reveal to you the poor in your life right now, and where he'd like you to reach out.

THE LOCAL CHURCH

Matthew 19:21: Jesus answered [the rich young man], "If you want to be perfect, go, sell your possessions and give to the poor, and you will have treasure in heaven. Then come, follow me."

Luke 11:39–41: Then the Lord said to him [the Pharisee who had invited him for dinner], "Now then, you Pharisees clean the outside of the cup and dish, but inside you are full of greed and wickedness. You foolish people! Did not the one who made the outside make the inside also? But give what is inside the dish [or what you have] to the poor, and everything will be clean for you."

Luke 12:32–33: "Do not be afraid, little flock, for your Father has been pleased to give you the kingdom. Sell your possessions and give to the poor. Provide purses for yourselves that will not wear out, a treasure in heaven that will not be exhausted, where no thief comes near and no moth destroys."

Luke 14:12–14: Then Jesus said to his host, "When you give a luncheon or dinner, do not invite your friends, your brothers or relatives, or your rich neighbors; if you do, they may invite you back and so you will be repaid. But when you give a banquet, invite the poor, the crippled, the lame, the blind, and you will be blessed. Although they cannot repay you, you will be repaid at the resurrection of the righteous."

Acts 4:33–35: With great power the apostles continued to testify to the resurrection of the Lord Jesus, and much grace was upon them all. There were no needy persons among them. For from time to time those who owned lands or houses sold them, brought the money from the sales and put it at the apostles' feet, and it was distributed to anyone as he had need.

Acts 10:3–4: One day at about three in the afternoon he [Cornelius] had a vision. He distinctly saw an angel of God, who came to him and said, "Cornelius!"

Cornelius stared at him in fear. "What is it, Lord?" he asked.

The angel answered, "Your prayers and gifts to the poor have come up as a memorial offering before God."

1 Corinthians 13:3: If I give all I possess to the poor and surrender my body to the flames, but have not love, I gain nothing.

James 2:1–4: My brothers, as believers in our glorious Lord Jesus Christ, don't show favoritism. Suppose a man comes into your meeting wearing a gold ring and fine clothes, and a poor man in shabby clothes also comes in. If you show special attention to the man wearing fine clothes and say, "Here's a good seat for you," but say to the poor man, "You stand there" or "Sit on the floor by my feet," have you not discriminated among yourselves and become judges with evil thoughts?

THE COURTS AND LEGISLATURE

Exodus 23:6: "Do not deny justice to your poor people in their lawsuits."

Leviticus 19:15: "Do not pervert justice; do not show partiality to the poor or favoritism to the great, but judge your neighbor fairly."

Proverbs 22:22–23: Do not exploit the poor because they
   are poor
  and do not crush the needy in court,
 for the LORD will take up their case
  and will plunder those who plunder them.

Isaiah 10:1–3: Woe to those who make unjust laws,
  to those who issue oppressive decrees,
 to deprive the poor of their rights
  and withhold justice from the oppressed of my people,
 making widows their prey
  and robbing the fatherless.

Jeremiah 5:26–29: "Among my people are wicked men
  who lie in wait like men who snare birds
  and like those who set traps to catch men.
 Like cages full of birds,
  their houses are full of deceit;
 they have become rich and powerful
  and have grown fat and sleek.
 Their evil deeds have no limit;
  they do not plead the case of the fatherless to win it,

they do not defend the rights of the poor.
Should I not punish them for this?"
    declares the LORD.
"Should I not avenge myself
    on such a nation as this?"

HUNGER

Exodus 23:11: "During the seventh year let the land lie unplowed and unused. Then the poor among your people may get food from it, and the wild animals may eat what they leave. Do the same with your vineyard and your olive grove."

Leviticus 19:10: "Do not go over your vineyard a second time or pick up the grapes that have fallen. Leave them for the poor and the alien. I am the LORD your God."

Leviticus 23:22: "When you reap the harvest of your land, do not reap to the very edges of your field or gather the gleanings of your harvest. Leave them for the poor and the alien. I am the LORD your God."

LENDING AND DEBT

Exodus 22:25: "If you lend money to one of my people among you who is needy, do not be like a moneylender; charge him no interest."

Deuteronomy 24:10–13: When you make a loan of any kind to your neighbor, do not go into his house to get what he is offering as a pledge. Stay outside and let the man to whom you are making the loan bring the pledge out to you. If the man is poor, do not go to sleep with his pledge in your possession. Return his cloak to him by sunset so that he may sleep in it. Then he will thank you, and it will be regarded as a righteous act in the sight of the LORD your God.

Proverbs 22:7: The rich rule over the poor,
    and the borrower is servant to the lender.

Proverbs 28:8: He who increases his wealth by
    exorbitant interest
    amasses it for another, who will be kind to the poor.

EMPLOYMENT

Deuteronomy 24:14–15: Do not take advantage of a hired man who is poor and needy, whether he is a brother Israelite or an alien living in one of your towns. Pay him his wages each day before sunset, because he is poor and is counting on it. Otherwise he may cry to the LORD against you, and you will be guilty of sin.

THE SOCIAL CONTRACT

Leviticus 25:35: "If one of your countrymen becomes poor and is unable to support himself among you, help him as you would an alien or a temporary resident, so he can continue to live among you."

Leviticus 25:39: "If one of your countrymen becomes poor among you and sells himself to you, do not make him work as a slave."

Deuteronomy 15:7–8: If there is a poor man among your brothers in any of the towns of the land that the LORD your God is giving you, do not be hardhearted or tightfisted toward your poor brother. Rather be openhanded and freely lend him whatever he needs. Be careful not to harbor this wicked thought: "The seventh year, the year for canceling debts, is near," so that you do not show ill will toward your needy brother and give him nothing. He may then appeal to the LORD against you, and you will be found guilty of sin. Give generously to him and do so without a grudging heart; then because of this the LORD your God will bless you in all your work and in everything you put your hand to. There will always be poor people in the land. Therefore I command you to be openhanded toward your brothers and toward the poor and needy in your land.

Proverbs 13:23: A poor man's field may produce abundant food,
    but injustice sweeps it away.

Proverbs 14:20: The poor are shunned even by their neighbors,
   but the rich have many friends.

Proverbs 31:9: Speak up and judge fairly;
   defend the rights of the poor and needy.

Ecclesiastes 5:8: If you see the poor oppressed in a district, and justice and rights denied, do not be surprised at such things; for one official is eyed by a higher one, and over them both are others higher still.

THE FAMILY COMPACT

Leviticus 25:25: "If one of your countrymen becomes poor and sells some of his property, his nearest relative is to come and redeem what his countryman has sold."

Leviticus 25:47–49: "If an alien or a temporary resident among you becomes rich and one of your countrymen becomes poor and sells himself to the alien living among you or to a member of the alien's clan, he retains the right of redemption after he has sold himself. One of his relatives may redeem him: An uncle or a cousin or any blood relative in his clan may redeem him. Or if he prospers, he may redeem himself."

AND THEN GOD SAID THIS ...

Psalm 14:6: You evildoers frustrate the plans of the poor,
   but the LORD is their refuge.

Psalm 22:26: The poor will eat and be satisfied;
   they who seek the LORD will praise him—
   may your hearts live forever!

Psalm 34:6: This poor man called, and the LORD heard him;
   he saved him out of all his troubles.

Psalm 35:10: My whole being will exclaim,

"Who is like you, O Lord?
You rescue the poor from those too strong for them,
the poor and needy from those who rob them."

Psalm 37:14–15: The wicked draw the sword
and bend the bow
to bring down the poor and needy,
to slay those whose ways are upright.
But their swords will pierce their own hearts,
and their bows will be broken.

Psalm 72:4: He will defend the afflicted among the people
and save the children of the needy;
he will crush the oppressor.

Psalm 112:1–9: Praise the Lord.

Blessed is the man who fears the Lord,
who finds great delight in his commands.

His children will be mighty in the land;
the generation of the upright will be blessed.
Wealth and riches are in his house,
and his righteousness endures forever.
Even in darkness light dawns for the upright,
for the gracious and compassionate and righteous man.
Good will come to him who is generous and lends freely,
who conducts his affairs with justice.
Surely he will never be shaken;
a righteous man will be remembered forever.
He will have no fear of bad news;
his heart is steadfast, trusting in the Lord.
His heart is secure, he will have no fear;
in the end he will look in triumph on his foes.
He has scattered abroad his gifts to the poor,
his righteousness endures forever;
his horn will be lifted high in honor.

Psalm 140:12: I know that the LORD secures justice for the poor
and upholds the cause of the needy.

Proverbs 14:21: He who despises his neighbor sins,
but blessed is he who is kind to the needy.

Proverbs 14:31: He who oppresses the poor shows contempt for
their Maker,
but whoever is kind to the needy honors God.

Proverbs 19:17: He who is kind to the poor lends to the LORD,
and he will reward him for what he has done.

Proverbs 21:13: If a man shuts his ears to the cry of the poor,
he too will cry out and not be answered.

Proverbs 22:2: Rich and poor have this in common:
The LORD is the Maker of them all.

Proverbs 22:9: A generous man will himself be blessed,
for he shares his food with the poor.

Proverbs 22:16: He who oppresses the poor to increase
his wealth
and he who gives gifts to the rich — both come
to poverty.

Proverbs 28:3: A ruler who oppresses the poor
is like a driving rain that leaves no crops.

Proverbs 28:27: He who gives to the poor will lack nothing,
but he who closes his eyes to them receives many curses.

Proverbs 29:7: The righteous care about justice for the poor,
but the wicked have no such concern.

Proverbs 29:14: If a king judges the poor with fairness,
his throne will always be secure.

Proverbs 30:11 – 14: There are those who curse their fathers

and do not bless their mothers;
those who are pure in their own eyes
and yet are not cleansed of their filth;
those whose eyes are ever so haughty,
whose glances are so disdainful;
those whose teeth are swords
and whose jaws are set with knives
to devour the poor from the earth,
the needy from among mankind.

Proverbs 31:20: She [a wife of noble character] opens her arms
to the poor
and extends her hands to the needy.

Isaiah 3:13 – 15: The LORD takes his place in court;
he rises to judge the people.
The LORD enters into judgment
against the elders and leaders of his people:
"It is you who have ruined my vineyard;
the plunder from the poor is in your houses.
What do you mean by crushing my people
and grinding the faces of the poor?"
declares the LORD, the LORD Almighty.

Isaiah 32:7 – 8: The scoundrel's methods are wicked,
he makes up evil schemes
to destroy the poor with lies,
even when the plea of the needy is just.
But the noble man makes noble plans,
and by noble deeds he stands.

Isaiah 58:6 – 7: "Is not this the kind of fasting I have chosen:
to loose the chains of injustice
and untie the cords of the yoke,
to set the oppressed free
and break every yoke?

Is it not to share your food with the hungry
　　and to provide the poor wanderer with shelter—
when you see the naked, to clothe him,
　　and not to turn away from your own flesh and blood?"

Zechariah 7:10: Do not oppress the widow or the fatherless, the alien or the poor. In your hearts do not think evil of each other.

ACKNOWLEDGMENTS

To those we invited to journey with us to Africa (but couldn't include in the book for simplicity's sake), thank you—Jennifer, Erin, Elysa, Anna, Betsy, and Erin W.

To the good folks at Zondervan who caught the vision, particularly Angela Scheff—you rock!—and Dirk Buursma. This wouldn't have sounded half so good without you.

To all who prayed for us and who supported the cause for "Sam's School"—may God continue to bless you.

To Will, Jake, and Gwynnie, for keeping things going on the home front—we love you.

This is Gertrude. She introduced herself by giving the warmest hugs.

Mealie pap, or just "pap," as everyone calls it in Swaziland, consists of water, salt, and mealie meal. It's very similar to grits, although they add sorghum in Swaziland to sweeten the dish.

These girls were just so much fun to be with. They were so seemingly carefree and just happy, despite spending their lives at Big Bend.

A grandmother (*gogo*) washing dishes at the first carepoint.

Inside this dusty hut lives a paralyzed woman. She sits inside all day and weaves rugs out of candy wrappers. She didn't say a word to us when we were there, but we prayed, and God was there.

Dennis is one of the kindest people I've ever met. Here's Dennis with a child overlooking the very dusty Big Bend.

This photo illustrates the pure friendliness of Swaziland. Most of the people we encountered there were warm, smiling people.

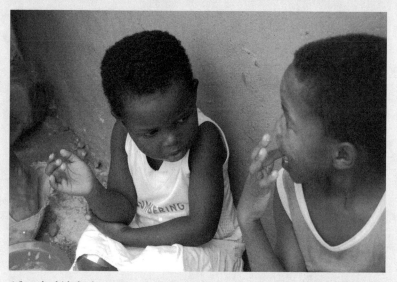

After the kids had prayed and received their food, they separated into different groups. They sat, chatted, and ate. It was very much like a cafeteria, except we were beneath the hot African sun.

This is a child whom I believe will succeed in overcoming the life she is in now. She has that look in her eyes—that look of gentle power.

Big Bend goes on for miles and miles. The land is dusty and barren, and this is where many of the children we visited are forced to live their daily lives.

This is a picture of friendship. A friendship built on the need to care for the poor. Tom and Pastor Walter are prime examples on how to help those in need and to keep on laughing.

Behind this child is dust. Dust is everywhere. And somehow he manages to keep smiling.

This little boy had such a fun spirit. He played soccer almost the entire time we were at the first carepoint.

It was amazing to see children so happy over something as small as candy. But these kids were. I can't imagine being that appreciative of something so small.

After trying for over an hour, this little boy finally let me take a quick picture of him. I think the only reason he let me take it was because all the girls were dancing!

This is a portrait of sadness. This little girl smiled and laughed for much of our time at that carepoint, but I captured this shot of her when she wasn't expecting it.

A typical "kitchen" at a carepoint

This photo shows that boys will be boys, wherever they may be.

An image of power. Power to succeed and overcome the life you've been forced into.

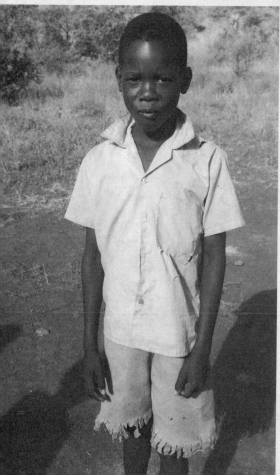

It was obvious this particular boy was embarrassed about the state of his clothing. He was a child who felt like he had to put down other children. But you can see the hurt behind his eyes.

It was fascinating to see children at such young ages taking care of themselves. Even the child pictured here, who seemed to be not quite two years old, fed himself and washed his dish.

We nicknamed this little girl "the tickler." She was so play-ful, and her favorite thing to do was go around and tickle everyone in the group.